# FACTS AT YOUR FINGERTIPS

# ANCIENT
# MESOPOTAMIA

BROWN
BEAR
BOOKS

**Published by Brown Bear Books Limited**

An imprint of:
The Brown Reference Group Ltd
68 Topstone Road
Redding
Connecticut 06896
USA

www.brownreference.com

Library of Congress Cataloging-in-Publication Data
available upon request

ISBN-13 978-1-933834-57-3

**Editorial Director:** Lindsey Lowe
**Managing Editor:** Tim Cooke
**Design Manager:** David Poole
**Designer:** Sarah Williams
**Picture Manager:** Sophie Mortimer
**Picture Researcher:** Sean Hannaway
**Text Editor:** Anita Dalal
**Indexer:** Indexing Specialists (UK) Ltd

Printed in the United States of America

# CONTENTS

# INTRODUCTION

**This book is** about the region known as Mesopotamia—the land between the Tigris and Euphrates Rivers—and the Ancient Near East. It covers the present-day country of Iraq as well as parts of Iran, Turkey, Syria, Lebanon, and Israel. The region is varied in geography and climate, ranging from deserts to forested mountains and fertile river plains.

## Early Peoples

More than 12,000 years ago, people in this region were among the first to change from a hunting-and-gathering, wandering lifestyle to settled farming communities. Many of the plants and animals on which modern agriculture is based were first domesticated (brought under human control) in the Near East.

The first cities in the world also emerged in Mesopotamia, by about 4000 BCE, and influenced the surrounding cultures. The ancient Greeks and Romans learned from Mesopotamian civilization, and passed on their cultural heritage to Europe. For this reason, Mesopotamia has been called the "cradle of civilization."

## War zone

Throughout its history, Mesopotamia has been a battlefield between warring empires and peoples. Many wars have been fought in the region from earliest times. The first kings, dating from about 3000 BCE, were originally leaders chosen by the people to defend city-states in times of war. By 2300 BCE, kings had become permanent heads of state, attending not only to military matters, but also to the welfare of the population.

Rulers were thought to be responsible to the gods, even though some of them, such as the Assyrian, Babylonian, and Persian kings, ruled vast empires. The empire of Darius III was conquered by Alexander the Great in 331 BCE. From then on, the civilization of the ancient Near East went into decline, to be replaced by the newly powerful Hellenistic (Greek-speaking culture)

## Rise and fall

This book traces the development of the earliest peoples of the region, through village to city life. It describes the cultural and technological developments which gave birth to civilization, and it charts the rise and fall of the great kingdoms and empires of the Near East. These began with the reign of the Semitic king Sargon of Agade (2334–279 BCE) and ended with the Persian dynasty.

Much of the evidence for the colorful history of Mesopotamia and the surrounding cultures comes from archeological excavations. Throughout the book, special pages focus on the contribution of outstanding sites, photographs show the heritage that we have today, and drawings illustrate how the sites may have looked in their original form. In addition, maps show how the empires grew and then faded, to be replaced by others. Both text and illustrations help to tell the full and fascinating story of the rise and fall of Mesopotamia, the "cradle of civilization."

**Abbreviations used in this book:**
BCE = Before Common Era (also known as BC)
CE = Common Era (also known as AD)
c. = circa (about)
ft = feet; in = inches;
cm = centimeter; m = meter; km = kilometer

*Cuneiform (wedge-shaped) writing carved on a relief of an Assyrian making a thumbs-up gesture.*

# TIMELINES

| | 12,000 BCE | 10,000 BCE | 7000 BCE | 4000 BCE | 3000 BCE |
|---|---|---|---|---|---|
| **ARCHAEOLOGICAL Period** | EPI-PALEOLITHIC (MESOLITHIC) | PROTO-NEOLITHIC | ACERAMIC NEOLITHIC | NEOLITHIC | SUMERIAN / EARLY BRONZE AGE |

**TECHNICAL INVENTIONS**

- Hunting and gathering
- Dog domesticated
- Microlithic flint tools

- Villages
- Basketry
- Grain roasting
- Sheep herded
- Farming—grain crops
- Mud-bricks
- Weaving
- Pottery
- Early copper tools

- Ox plow
- Cattle domesticated
- Potter's wheel
- Baked mud-bricks
- Pottery kilns
- Irrigation
- Boats

- Cities
- Donkeys domesticated
- Carts
- Copper weapons
- Cylinder seals
- Cuneiform writing

- City-states
- Lost-wax method of casting metal
- Gold- and silversmithing

*Stone bird head from Nemrik, c.7500 BCE.*

*Flint arrowheads from Tell Brak.*

*Susa A bowl, c.4000 BCE.*

*Metal daggers from the Royal Cemetery of Ur, c.2600 BCE.*

**ART AND ARCHITECTURE**

- Round huts
- Plastered skulls
- Stone sculptures
- Rectangular houses
- Clay figurines
- Tripartite temples
- Walled cities
- Cone mosaics
- "Uruk Mona Lisa"
- "Warka vase"
- Palaces

**Major Events MESOPOTAMIA**

- End of Ice Age
- ✽ Shanidar Cave
- ✽ Zawi Chemi Shanidar
- <u>Hassuna, Samarra, Halaf, Ubaid</u>
- <u>Uruk</u>
- ✽ Tell Madhhur
- ✽ Ur
- <u>Jamdat Nasr</u>
- ✽ Mari
- <u>Early Dynastic</u>
- Nippur
- ✽ Uruk

**LEVANT**

- ✽ Mt Carmel
- ✽ Jericho
- <u>Halaf</u>
- <u>Ubaid</u>

*Printed stone mask from Nahal Hemar, c.10,000 BCE.*

**IRAN**

- ✽ Choga Mami

*Bronze and silver st[ag] from Alaca Huyuk, c.2300 BCE.*

**ANATOLIA**

- ✽ Chatal Hüyuk

**EGYPT**

- Pre-Dynastic

---

✽ denotes important site of the period     ▲ denotes a king     words <u>underlined</u> are historical periods

| 2500 BCE | 2000 BCE | 1500 BCE | 1000 BCE | 750 BCE | 600 BCE | 300 BCE |
|---|---|---|---|---|---|---|
| AKKADIAN | MIDDLE BRONZE AGE | LATE BRONZE AGE | | IRON AGE | | |

Armies

Horse domesticated
Law codes
Sumerian King List
Hammurabi's law code

Glazed pottery
Glass
Chariots

Cavalry
Alphabet—Aramaic writing
Battering-ram
Siege engine

*Faience mask from Tell al-Rimah, c.1350 BCE.*

*Choga Zanbil ziggurat, c.1200 BCE.*

*Samarian ivory, c.900 BCE.*

*Horse head on a relief from Dur-Sharrukin, c.710 BCE.*

Ziggurats

Glazed, molded bricks

Kudurru stones

Ivory carving

Royal library, Nineveh

Hanging Gardens, Babylon

Kings of Agade
▲ Sargon
▲ Naram-Sin

Third Dynasty of Ur
Isin–Larsa

Assyrian
▲ Shamshi-Adad

(Amorites)
Mittani

Kassites

Old Babylonian

❋ Ashur

(Aramaeans)

Middle Babylonian

Middle Assyrian

❋ Nineveh

Medes

Late Babylonian

❋ Kalhu
Late Assyrian
▲ Tiglath-Pileser
▲ Sargon
▲ Sennacherib
▲ Esarhaddon
▲ Ashurbanipal
❋ Babylon
New Babylonians

Persians

▲ Nabopolassar

▲ Nebuchadrezzar

❋ Ebla

Mittani

(Sea Peoples)
(Philistines)
(Israelites)

Israel and Judah
David
Solomon

Assyrian victory

Exile of Jews to Babylon

*Head of blue paste from Persepolis, c.450 BCE.*

*Bronze weight from Kalhu, c.700 BCE.*

Persians—Cyrus, Darius

❋ Susa

(Hurrians)

Hittites

Lydians

New Kingdom

Amarna Letters

Ramesses III

(Sea Peoples)

Cambyses

**7**

# EARLY PEOPLES

**The earliest evidence** of a human presence in ancient Mesopotamia—the region around the Tigris and Euphrates rivers—dates as far back as 85,000 BCE. During the Old Stone Age (also known as the Paleolithic Age), two separate groups of hominids existed. *Homo sapiens*—the ancestors of human beings—lived side-by-side with *Homo neanderthalensis* (Neanderthals, who have long been extinct). Both these groups were hunter–gatherers. They were semi-nomadic peoples who lived by hunting wild animals and collecting wild plants and anything else they could eat. For shelter, they used caves. Two cave dwellings have been discovered at Mount Carmel (in present-day Israel) and Shanidar (present-day Iraq).

Human development was interrupted during the Ice Ages, when temperatures fell and ice sheets spread from the poles to cover far more of the land. After the last major Ice Age reached a peak around 20,000 years ago, and the ice began to recede, *Homo sapiens* began to lead a more settled life in West Asia. They grew crops and kept animals. The move from hunting and gathering to living in one place and growing crops took many thousands of years. Gradually between 11,000 and 9000 BCE, people started to live in small communities of settled villages.

## The Neolithic Revolution

When the last Ice Age ended, temperatures rose all over Earth. This led to the evolution of different plants and probably the extinction of several animals, especially larger animals such as the woolly mammoth. The changes in the environment led to what is known as the Neolithic Revolution (Neolithic means "New Stone Age"). The Neolithic marked the change in behavior, as the hunter-gatherers moved to permanent villages.

The earliest settlements that archeologists have discovered are in present-day Palestine and the upper Euphrates valley in present-day Syria. From the physical evidence, it appears as though the villages developed separately and were not linked in any way.

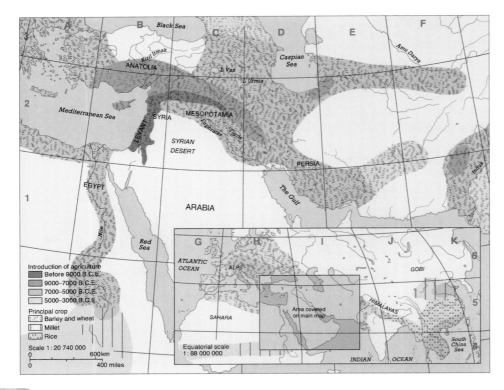

*Early agriculture. Barley and wheat were first cultivated in the foothills of northern Mesopotamia between about 11,000 and 9000 BCE. By about 5000 BCE, these crops were grown in the Caucasus to the north, in Egypt to the south, to the west in Anatolia (Turkey) and southeastern Europe, and eastward in Iran and even India. In China and southeast Asia, rice and millet were being cultivated.*

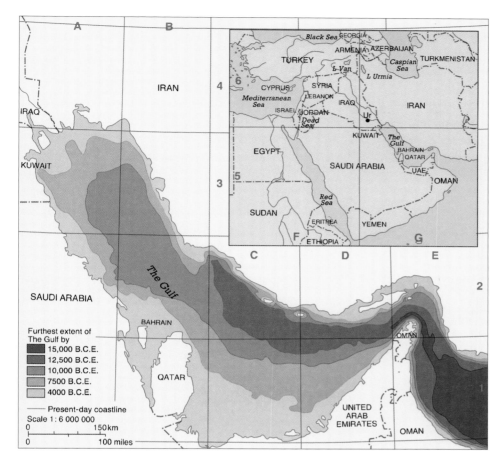

The changing shape of the Gulf. The Gulf has been growing in size since 15,000 BCE, when sea levels were about 330 feet (100 m) lower than today. As the last Ice Age ended, sea levels rose with the warmer temperatures. Since 4000 BCE, sea levels have remained almost the same, but silting from the Tigris and Euphrates rivers has significantly changed the coastline. These maps show the boundaries of present-day countries.

## Stone Technology

As the settled communities produced new crops, they needed different tools to help them to prepare the land or to turn the harvest into food. For example, certain grains needed to be ground to produce flour, and early humans had to develop tools for grinding. They made most of their tools from flint or other hard stone that could be easily found and then shaped to create sharp edges or blunt hammers. The tools were fashioned into different shapes for chipping, flaking, or "pecking."

Smaller flints began to appear toward the end of the Paleolithic Age. They are known as microliths and were made in different shapes. These tools were better than those of the Old Stone Age, because they were sharper and more efficient than the older, larger tools. The tools show that people were already collecting grains,

### Near East Paleolithic and Mesolithic Cultures

**Lower Paleolithic 85,000–60,000 BCE** – Acheulean Culture. Site: Shanidar Cave (Base), Iraq.

**Middle Paleolithic 60,000–35,000 BCE** – Mousterian Culture. Site: Shanidar Cave (Layers D,C), Iraq. 40,000 BCE – *Homo sapiens* appears

**Upper Paleolithic 35,000–18,000 BCE** – Baradostian Cultures. Sites: Kebara (Layer D), Israel; Zarzi, Iraq.

**Epi-Paleolithic (Mesolithic) 18,000–12,000 BCE** – Zarzian Culture

**End of the last Ice Age** Sites: Kebara (Layers C, B), Israel; M'Lefaat, Iraq; Karim Shahir, Iraq; Shanidar Cave (Layer B), Iraq; Zawi Chemi Shanidar (B), Iraq; Mt Carmel, Israel.

although on their own they do not prove that the people were yet growing the plants themselves. Some tools found at Mount Carmel were set in bone sickle-handles and were used as curved cutting tools.

# Shanidar

**Shanidar Cave is** one of the earliest known hominid settlements. The site is located near the Great Zab River in the Zagros Mountains of Iraqi Kurdistan. Archeological evidence suggests that as early as 100,000 BCE, small groups of Neanderthal people moved into the cave during the harsh winter months. We know that they hunted wild sheep, pigs, cattle, and goats.

From analysis of bones found in the cave, it is clear that some inhabitants were killed by rock falls. Other skeletons have been found with pollen deposits nearby, suggesting that the Neanderthals may have buried their dead, sometimes with flowers. The stone tools found in the cave date to the Middle Paleolithic Mousterian Culture.

The cave was also used by modern humans (*Homo sapiens*), who arrived at Shanidar in about 40,000 BCE. Their arrival is indicated by tools in the cave that are more advanced than those of the Neanderthals, who died out by 33,000 BCE. There is no evidence of human occupation of the cave for a very long period, between 28,000 and 12,000 BCE.

Later tools found in the cave were made from obsidian—a black, glasslike volcanic rock—which was not found locally. Their presence suggests that the cave dwellers were trading with people in southeast Turkey, the nearest source of obsidian.

The most recent skeletons found in the cave date from about 10,000 BCE. There were 26 skeletons, some of which were buried with grave goods. One skeleton belonged to a man who had had his arm cut off, possibly as the result of an injury or a disease.

## Zawi Chemi Shanidar

Located about 1.8 miles (3 km) from Shanidar Cave is Zawi Chemi Shanidar, the site of the first proper villages in Ancient Mesopotamia, such as Jarmo. The villagers used stone tools like those of the early cave dwellers, but they also had new types of tools. Again, they traded with other communities for the materials they used in tool making.

The villagers built circular huts with boulders taken from the river. These huts measured about 13 feet (4 m) in diameter, and archeologists have discovered huts from three different periods. The villages may have been used during the summer and then abandoned for the Shanidar Cave during the cold winters. From pollen samples, we know that the villagers harvested wild wheat and barley and also tried to sow their own domesticated crops. Bones from young animals found at the site show that sheep and goats were being herded from around 10,000 BCE; the people also hunted wild animals for meat.

Other interesting finds include a pile of eagles' wing bones and the skulls of 15 goats. These remains have led archeologists to think the villagers practiced some kind of religious ceremonies at Zawi Chemi Shanidar. The area was settled at the same time as many of the ancient sites in the Levant, but archeologists think they were independent of each other.

*In Zawi Chemi Shanidar, men and women performed different tasks. By the campfire, male hunters sharpen flint to make spearheads, while another man returns from the forest with firewood. Outside the hut, women clean and scrape the hide from a red deer, which will be used for clothing or to make the roof of a hut. In the background are some of the villagers' domesticated goats and sheep.*

# THE FIRST FARMERS (11,000–9300 BCE)

**The development of** agriculture occurred in West Asia about 13,000 years ago. It was one of the first parts of the world where animals were domesticated and crops were cultivated. The wild ancestors of the animals and the grains had originated in the Levant region and in the hills that flanked the Syrian and the Mesopotamian plains.

## Grain Collection

The start of the Neolithic revolution in about 11,000 BCE is known as the Natufian period of culture in the region, named for a site at Wadi an-Natuf. Sickles and grinding stones from the period found at Mount Carmel on the shores of the Mediterranean Sea indicate that cereals were an important element of the daily diet. In Syria, at Ain Mallaha, excavations have revealed a number of bell-shaped storage pits. They were lined with plaster and used to store grain. At Mureybet, in northern Syria, pits dug into the earth were used to roast grain. It is not possible to tell whether the stored and roasted cereals were gathered or cultivated.

## Grain Cultivation

The Natufian people ate wild barley and two kinds of wheat, which we know grew in the wild in West Asia. We are fairly sure that einkorn wheat and emmer wheat provided the seeds from which the first domesticated crops were grown. Over successive generations, the people produced several different domestic varieties by selective planting and harvesting. The villagers learned how to increase the yield from crops such as barley so that they produced more seeds. The selection process helped people to produce more food, which they needed as their villages grew. By 8000 BCE, most of the settled villages in West Asia grew cereals.

## Animal Husbandry

Early humans developed ways to herd and then farm animals to supplement their diet of plants and seeds. The process of domestication took place in different parts of the world over many generations and was complicated and gradual. The dog was among the first animals to be

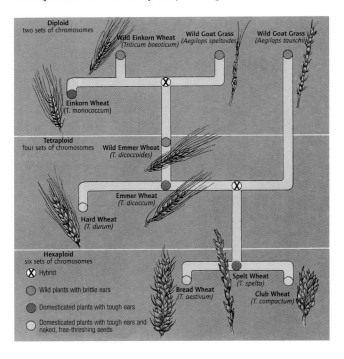

Stages in the domestication of wheat in West Asia. Emmer wheat was a natural hybrid (cross-bred offspring) of einkorn wheat and goat grass. Further selective breeding then helped to produce wheat plants ideal for harvesting and threshing.

## Origin of common farm animals

| Domesticated animal | Wild ancestor | Region | Date |
|---|---|---|---|
| Dog | Wolf | West Asia | c.11,000 BCE |
| Goat | Bezoar goat | West Asia | c.8500 BCE |
| Sheep | Asiatic mouflon | West Asia | c.8000 BCE |
| Pig | Wild boar | West Asia | c.7500 BCE |
| Cattle | Auroch | West Asia | c.7000 BCE |
| Cat | Wild cat | West Asia | c.7000 BCE |
| Chicken | Red jungle fowl | China | c.6000 BCE |
| Llama | Guanaco | Andes | c.5000 BCE |
| Donkey | Wild ass | West Asia | c.4000 BCE |
| Horse | Tarpan | Southern Russia | c.4000 BCE |
| Camel | Wild camel | Arabia/ South Central Asia | c.3000 BCE |
| Guinea pig | Cavy | Peru | c.2000 BCE |
| Rabbit | Wild rabbit | Spain | c.1000 BCE |
| Turkey | Wild turkey | Mexico | c.300 BCE |

domesticated—from the wild wolf—probably to help people hunt, but possibly also as food. At Ain Mallaha, a skeleton of a puppy was buried in a woman's grave in about 10,000 BCE Among other native animals of West Asia that were domesticated were wild cattle (aurochs), which became cows, and mouflons, which became sheep.

From remains discovered at Natufian sites that include Mount Carmel and Abu Hureyra in Syria, we know that early humans ate wild animals, such as gazelle, boar, and deer. The large numbers of bones from young animals would suggest that animals were herded and killed on a selective basis.

*Settlements and farmers. After the last Ice Age, people began to establish villages in areas of good rainfall—over 8 inches (20 cm) a year—where cereals grew naturally and animals were plentiful. Such early village sites span the Fertile Crescent from the Levant through northern Syria to Kurdistan and Iraq.*

## Grain-gathering cultures during the Mesolithic period

**18,000–11,000 BCE** KEBARAN culture
Site: Kebara, Israel

**15,000 BCE** First evidence of circular huts and mortars
Site: Ain Gev, Israel.

**12,000 BCE** End of last Ice Age (Pleistocene)

**11,000 BCE** Seasonal or permanent settlement in northern Mesopotamia
Site: Zawi Chemi Shanidar

**11,000–9300 BCE** NATUFIAN culture
Seasonal or permanent settlement, with milling and roasting of grain
Sites: Mt. Carmel, Israel; Ain Mallaha, Syria; Beidha, Jordan; Abu Hureyra, Syria

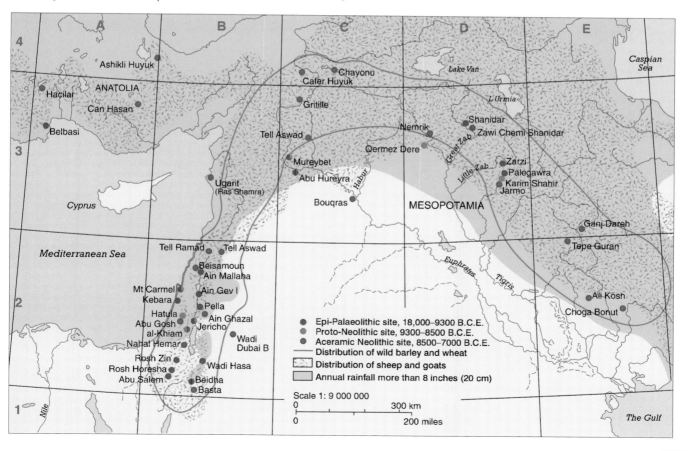

# BUILDERS AND TRADERS

**Buildings constructed from** unbaked mud bricks first appeared around 8,000 BCE. People used the bricks because they were cheap and easy to make from the muddy banks of the great rivers; mud was also easier to use than stone. The earliest bricks date from the Proto-Neolithic period. They were made by hand and looked a little like a loaf of bread with a flat bottom and a rounded top. Once people learned how to make mud bricks with straight sides, houses became rectangular. That happened much later. Mud bricks tend to fall apart over time, so it is very exciting when archeologists find any ancient bricks that survive.

## Jericho

Jericho, which lies in the Jordan valley, was inhabited from 9,000 BCE. The earliest-known mud bricks, made by hand and shaped like a cigar, were used there to build round huts. Around 8,000 BCE, a massive stone wall and a large ditch were built to protect the huts. A large stone tower that incorporated an internal staircase was probably also used to defend the settlement. Jericho is mentioned in the Bible; the Israelite leader Joshua marches his army around the city until the walls collapse.

## Using Metals and Clay

About 8500 BCE, major changes arrived with the use of metal. In Chayonu, in present-day Turkey, more than 100 copper beads, pins, and tools have been excavated. The source of the copper is unknown. It may have been extracted locally rather than smelted. Copper beads have also been discovered at Ali Kosh in the Zagros Mountains. The Zagros Mountains were a rich source of minerals.

At Ganj Dareh, to the north of Ali Kosh, the buildings were rectangular-shaped and built of long, handmade mud bricks. The site has also revealed many human and animal figurines (small figures) made from clay. Pottery vessels have also been found at Ganj Dareh.

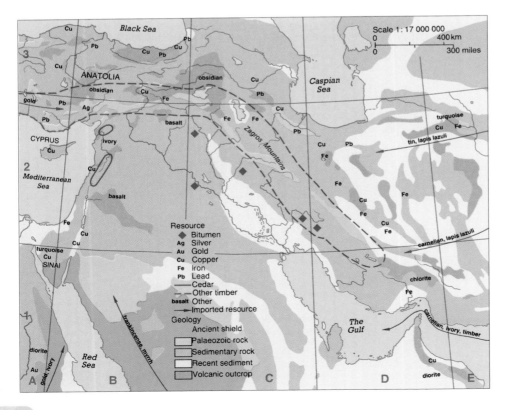

LEFT: Raw materials and trade. The Zagros Mountains were rich in minerals and wood. Copper came from Sinai; obsidian and metals from Anatolia. Mesopotamia had bitumen deposits, but lacked any other resources. Finding the source of a metal or stone helps us understand the development of trade.

RIGHT: The modern city of Meybod in Iran. Like settlements throughout Mesopotamia and its neighbors, Meybod is largely built from traditional mud bricks, which have been used for construction in the region for some 10,000 years.

At Mureybet, at the western end of the Fertile Crescent, four pots have been discovered in an ancient house. These pots are remarkable because they were lightly fired, or baked at a high temperature to strengthen them. The pots date from 8000 BCE, 500 years earlier than other fired pottery, and mark a new stage in technological development.

## Trade

Jericho was an oasis town with around 1,500 inhabitants. Its fortifications suggest that it had grown wealthy, probably as a regional trading center. Its merchants traded salt and bitumen from the nearby Dead Sea, cowrie shells from the Red Sea, as well as turquoise and copper from the Sinai Peninsula, and obsidian from Anatolia. The black volcanic glass obsidian was highly prized because it could be used to make much sharper cutting edges than flint. It is particularly valuable to archeologists as it comes from only a few sources, so it is relatively easy to trace its distribution along trade routes.

Archeologists think that traders from Jericho may have covered distances of up to 500 miles (800 km). It may be, however, that the traders only traveled short distances, and that goods passed through many hands on their journey. It is impossible to know for certain how wide the trade network was because many of the objects that were traded, such as animal skins, have long since perished.

### Clay-using cultures of the Near East

**9000–8500 BCE** Proto-Neolithic Period (Pre-Pottery Neolithic A)
Sites: Jericho, Jordan; Mureybet, Syria
First evidence of handmade bricks

---

**8500–7000 BCE** Aceramic Neolithic Period (Pre-Pottery Neolithic B)
Sites: Jericho, Jordan; Ain Ghazal, Jordan; Beidha, Jordan; Mureybet, Syria; Tell Abu Hurerya, Syria; Chayonu, Turkey; Jarmo, Iraq; Ganj Dareh, Iran. Use of handmade bricks; rectangular houses with plaster floors; clay modeling of animal and human figurines

---

**8000 BCE** Site: Mureybet, Syria
First evidence of fired pottery

# FIRST CIVILIZATION (7000–4000 BCE)

**By 7000 BCE,** the use of pottery was common across the Near East. As production grew more sophisticated, different types of pottery were made in different places. The many cultures that emerged at this time have been named after these distinctive pots. Most communities lived in settlements and relied on whatever rain fell to water their crops–usually in areas where rainfall averaged 10 inches (25 cm) per year. Over the next 3,000 years, village life became more organized as food production became more predictable thanks to irrigation.

## Early Pottery Cultures

Tell Hassuna in northern Iraq is an example of a village dating from the early pottery culture. The houses were rectangular-shaped and made from mud bricks. They were quite large as they had several rooms and courtyards. The villagers fired their pottery in large-domed kilns and they also wove wool. We know this because clay spindle whorls have been found at the site. The villagers also traded obsidian, turquoise, and seashells with people as far away as Anatolia and Sinai.

The Samarra and Choga Mami cultures both spread south from Hassuna. The early farmers of these cultures also relied on rainfall to water their crops, but this was not sufficient as the area was drier than Hassuna. Later farmers at Choga Mami built water channels to irrigate their fields and to make the most of the rainfall.

## Halaf Culture

The Halaf culture replaced the Hassuna culture. It was named after its site next to the Khabur

*Early pottery cultures, 7000–5400 BCE. In about 6000 BCE, the Hassuna culture overlapped the Samarra culture. About a thousand years later, the Halaf culture spread through the Zagros Mountains to northern Syria. The Ubaid culture developed in Sumer in southern Mesopotamia.*

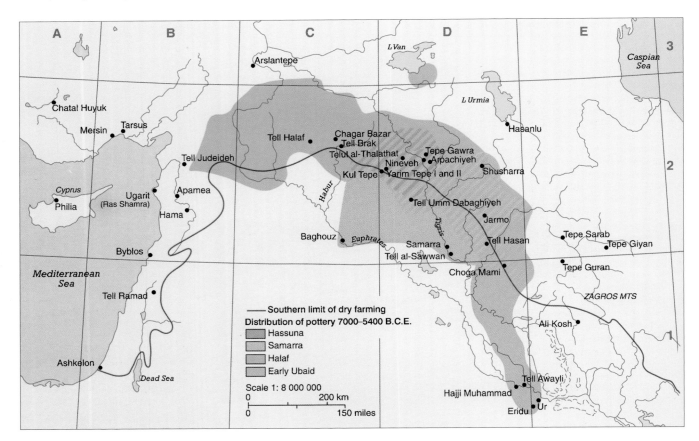

Southern limit of dry farming
Distribution of pottery 7000–5400 B.C.E.
- Hassuna
- Samarra
- Halaf
- Early Ubaid

Scale 1: 8 000 000
0   200 km
0   150 miles

River in Syria. The Halaf people lived in domed, circular huts made from mud bricks. The huts were called "tholoi." Halaf culture is notable for its pottery, which was beautifully painted. By 5500 BCE, the northern Halaf culture came into contact with the Ubaid culture.

## Ubaid Culture

The Ubaid culture lasted for more than a thousand years. It developed in the south of Mesopotamia and produced sophisticated buildings. At Eridu in Sumer, a number of temples were built. They may have been constructed to honor the water god, Enki. The Ubaid people buried their dead in graves made from mud bricks. Archeologists have discovered a cemetery with 200 rectangular-shaped graves in it. Their homes were made up of a central room with two rows of rooms on either side. The people traded far and wide.

Their distinctive pottery from the Late Ubaid has been found as far away as the Gulf region in present-day Saudi Arabia, Bahrain, and Qatar.

### Pottery Cultures 7000–4000 B.C.E.

**7000 B.C.E.** Proto-Hassuna

**6800 B.C.E.** Hassuna
Sites: Hassuna, Iraq; Tell Umm Dabaghiyeh, Iraq

**6500 B.C.E.** Samarra
Sites: Tel al-Sawwan, Iraq; Choga Mami, Iraq

**6000 B.C.E.** Halaf (Early)
Sites: Tell Halaf, Syria; Arpachiyeh, Iraq; Yarim Tepe, Iraq

**5900 B.C.E.** Ubaid (Early)
Site: Tell Halaf, Syria

**5400 B.C.E.** Ubaid (Late)
Site: Eridu, Iraq

*This pottery jar was made in the Late Ubaid period. The simple style of decoration of Ubaid pottery is one of the main ways archaeologists use to trace the extent of Ubaid influence. The pottery has been found as far down the Gulf as Saudi Arabia, Qatar, and the United Arab Emirates.*

# Tell Madhhur

Tell Madhhur is located in present-day eastern Iraq, close to the border with Iran. The area has now been flooded, because of the construction of a nearby dam, but before the area was flooded, the ancient site was excavated by archeologists.

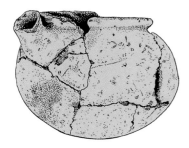

*A spouted jar, for storing and pouring liquids, was found in the kitchen of the house at Tell Madhhur. Similar vessels have been found at other sites. Most pots in the house were handmade, but some may have been finished on a wheel.*

*Among the 78 pottery items found in the house was this small painted cup or bowl. Pottery of all shapes and sizes was found. Some of the grain-storage jars were enormous and could hold as much as 24 gallons (109 liters).*

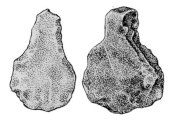

*Not all of the items found at Tell Madhhur were made of baked clay. These stone hoes were made of chipped flint. They would have been attached to a wooden handle by bitumen and a cord. Only stone or clay products survived the fire.*

The archeological team learned from their excavations that the buildings of Tell Madhhur had been constructed from mud that was baked hard by the sun. There were about 12 houses in total and they were built on a mound. In the center of the mound was a large house that dated from about 4000 BCE, during the Late Ubaid period. The only part of the house that remained was the walls. These survived because, although the house had once been burned by fire, people had filled it with soil. In the soil were found many everyday objects that would have been used inside the house. These included pottery vessels, clay spindle whorls, and stone hoes.

### "Tripartite" Architecture

At the heart of the house was a long central room, which was used as the main living area. On either side of the room were a series of smaller rooms. This type of design was typical of the Ubaid period and was known as "tripartite," because the house was made up of three areas; the central room and the two sides. Tripartite houses have been found at known Ubaid sites such as Tepe Gawra in northern Iraq.

This type of architectural structure was not just used for houses, but also for the construction of temples. At Tepe Gawra, three temples were built in this tripartite style. Others were built at Eridu and Uruk. The origins of this style of architecture are unclear, but it became the dominant form of Near Eastern temple architecture. It was used over a period of almost 2000 years in the building of tripartite temples in an area stretching from southern Mesopotamia to northern Syria.

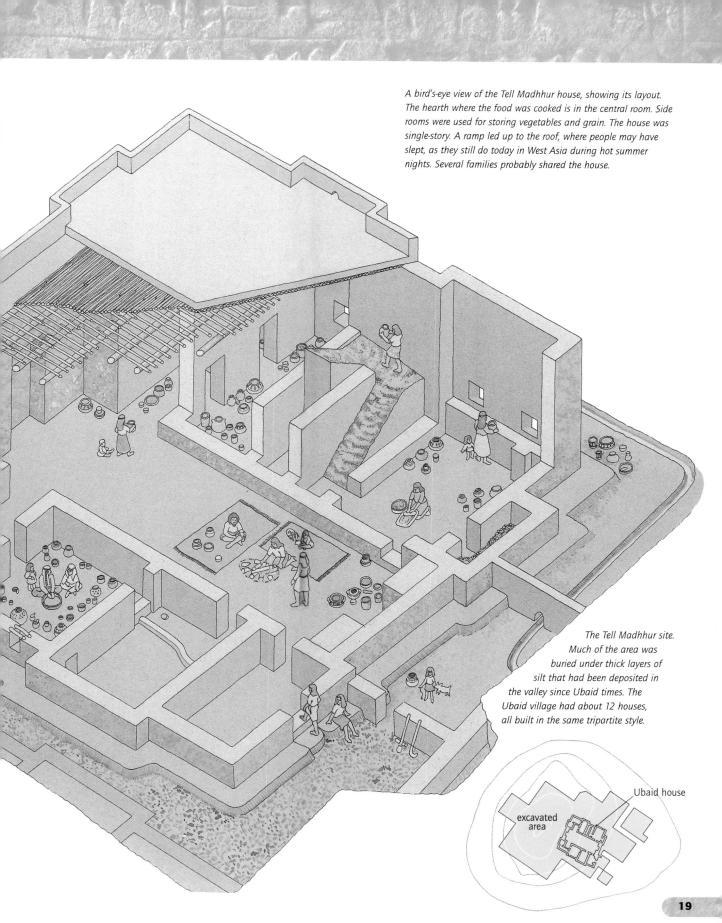

A bird's-eye view of the Tell Madhhur house, showing its layout. The hearth where the food was cooked is in the central room. Side rooms were used for storing vegetables and grain. The house was single-story. A ramp led up to the roof, where people may have slept, as they still do today in West Asia during hot summer nights. Several families probably shared the house.

The Tell Madhhur site. Much of the area was buried under thick layers of silt that had been deposited in the valley since Ubaid times. The Ubaid village had about 12 houses, all built in the same tripartite style.

Ubaid house

excavated area

# BIRTH OF THE CITY (4000–3000 BCE)

**Cities started to** appear in the region of southern Mesopotamia around 4000 BCE, before anywhere else in the world. Jericho and Catal Hüyuk had been early versions of proto-cities. They had city walls and housing that was closely spaced together, but they were just two isolated examples of early urban living. Cities, according to current definitions, date from the later Uruk period.

The change from village life to city life took place gradually between 4300 and 3450 BCE. People stopped working as farmers and began to live closer together in larger communities. People started to build temples at religious centers. They settled close to the Euphrates

*Ancient ruins stand above the Euphrates River in modern Syria. The river's broad plain was home to the first cities, which relied on the Euphrates for irrigation to water their fields and for the mud from which their buildings were constructed.*

River and the change in the river's course may help to explain why the density of settlements changed. During the Early and Middle Uruk periods, the northern region around Nippur was well populated. In contrast, during the Late Uruk period, most people settled in southern Mesopotamia. During the later Jamdat Nasr and Early Dynastic periods, many thousands settled in the city of Uruk and the neighboring area.

## Uruk-based cultures

**4300–3450 BCE** Early and Middle Uruk
Sites: Nippur region, Iraq; Uruk, Iraq

**3450–3000 BCE** Late Uruk
Sites: Uruk, Iraq

**3000 BCE** Jamdat Nasr
Sites: Uruk, Iraq; Jamdar Nasr, Iraq

## Specialized Labor

When people started to live in cities, they organized themselves very differently from village life. Instead of farming, people began to specialize in different trades. Many became craftspeople. During the Uruk period, they became better builders and built temples. Artistic achievement became more important and such activity increased across the Near East, arriving in Egypt around 3000 BCE. Trade then became increasingly important, because the artists needed materials for their work. Lapis lazuli, a semi-precious blue stone, was traded from Afghanistan, which was more than 1,250 miles (2000 km) away. Artists also worked with copper and its alloys and these became widely available. Archeologists think that professional smiths may well have been working the metals. Certainly, a metal industry was developing, with smiths working with gold, silver, copper, lead, and iron.

By 4000 BCE, farming had modernized. Farmers used the ox-plow to plow their fields and may have transported goods to the cities on carts pulled by oxen or even by boats across the marshes of southern Mesopotamia. Records of goods sent to Uruk were made by scribes (official writers) and are the earliest known written documents in existence.

*Towns of the Early–Middle Uruk period. More than half of the population of southern Mesopotamia lived in the fertile alluvial plains to the north and east of Nippur. The Euphrates and Tigris rivers were joined farther upstream.*

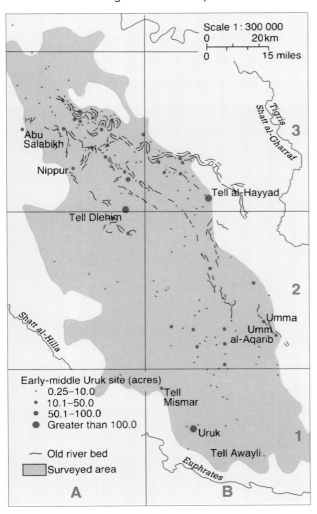

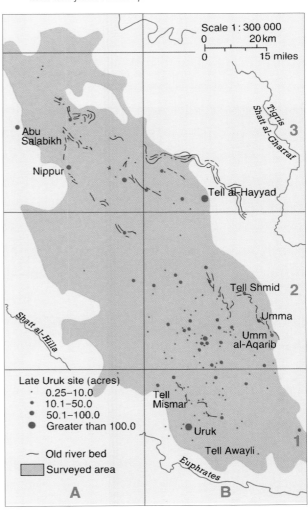

# Uruk

Uruk was one of the most magnificent cities in Sumer, in southern Mesopotamia. At its peak, in around 2900 BCE, it was

the largest city in the world, and it thrived for more than a thousand years after 4000 BCE. The site of Uruk lies close to modern-day Warka in Iraq, 156 miles (250 km) southeast of the capital, Baghdad.

Uruk was probably formed from two Ubaid settlements, Kullaba and Eanna. These settlements had temples to the sky god, Anu,

*A priestly procession enters the temple precinct at Uruk. The mighty columns of the monumental entrance are more than 6 feet (1.8 m) in diameter and are decorated with colored cones stuck into the plaster. A sheep and piles of dates are being brought to the goddess Inanna. The temples were much involved in the way that food production was organized.*

and the goddess of love, Inanna. Around 3000 BCE, the two sites were united to form a single city, Uruk. The city was big. It covered an area of 1,000 acres (400 hectares). To defend it, it was surrounded by a wall 6 miles (10 km) long. Uruk had its own king, Gilgamesh, who was famous in history and legend. He was the hero of the Sumerian story, *The Epic of Gilgamesh*.

## Temples and their Treasures

Uruk was an important religious center. At its heart were two tripartite temples, dedicated to Anu and Inanna. The temples were huge. They were built on a terrace and took up as much as one-third of the entire city. The temples were magnificent. Some parts of the temples were decorated with geometric designs that were made from thousands of small stone or clay cones painted black, red, and white. Staircases, positioned to the side, led to the roof, where special prayers were said. Inside

the temple were a stepped altar and a central table where offerings were burned.

The objects found in the temples were equally marvellous. Archeologists discovered a white marble mask of a woman's face in a pit near the Inanna temple. Almost life-sized, the mask may have had semi-precious stones (lapis lazuli) for eyes. The quality of the workmanship has led to its nickname, the *Mona Lisa of Uruk*. It may have been an image of Inanna.

Another object found at the Uruk temple site is an alabaster vessel that stands over 3 feet (1 m) high. The Warka vase has the earliest known religious scene in Mesopotamia carved on its façade in three bands. The top one shows food being offered to Inanna. The middle band has a procession of naked men, who may have been priests, carrying baskets of produce, while the bottom band shows sheep and grain. We think these carvings may show a festival to give thanks for good harvests.

This statuette of an unknown ruler of Uruk dates from the late 4th millennium BCE. Such figures were placed in temples as a sign of the ruler's devotion to the gods.

# STATES IN CONFLICT (3000–2350 BCE)

**In about 3000** BCE, the Uruk culture was replaced by the Early Dynastic I period. Sumer became a land of city–states. Each state was independent and was made up of a city and land. Water channels marked boundaries, but otherwise there were not any physical markers to show where one state ended and another started. The city–states often fought against each other. Kings started to come to power around this time.

## The City-State and its Leaders

The heart of the city-state, as with Uruk, was the temple, which was also the center of its economic wealth. It was the home of the patron god or goddess, and the temple owned large parts of the city's land, employing many people. The head priest was called *en*, meaning "lord."

Each city had governors ("ensis"), but free male citizens, who perhaps owned land, made decisions about the city. It was an early form

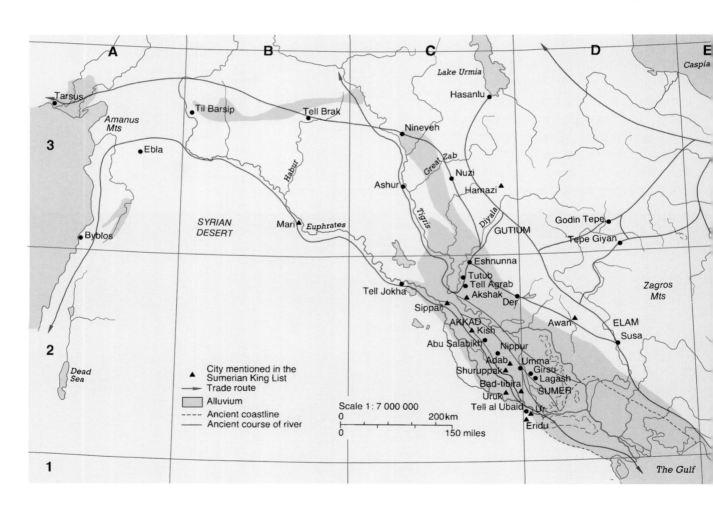

*Cities in the Sumerian King l...*
*Mesopotamia was divided into ...*
*regions. Sumer in the south stretc...*
*from Eridu, which was once on the G...*
*to Nippur. The King List listed the na...*
*of the rulers of the cities of Sumer ...*
*the length of their reig...*

of democracy. There was even a two-chamber early form of parliament. The upper house was made up of "elders," who were the city's most important citizens, and a lower house made up of "men," probably other landowners. If there was a problem, the assembly would gather to elect a leader, known as a "lugal." He had a lot of power. He was the commander in any wars, was the judge in disputes, and he also carried out rituals, such as blessing the harvests. He lived in an "egal," which meant "great house," although the word came to mean "palace."

Eventually, the lugal began to rival the temple lord in power and wealth. The position of lugal was made permanent and then, instead of being elected, the position became hereditary. The king saw himself as a representative of the gods, and as such, chosen by the gods. Part of the Sumerian kings' duty was to maintain the religious buildings in the city as a way of carrying out the will of the gods.

### The Sumerian King List

The Sumerian King List is an ancient cuneiform record of royal rulers. (Cuneiform was a system of writing that used wedge-shaped impressions pressed into soft clay). So far, at least 12 copies of the list have been found in Babylonia and at Susa and at Nineveh. The list records the names of all of the kings of the Early Dynastic period, many of whom are also mentioned in other cuneiform inscriptions. The King List records the rulers in consecutive order even though, in reality, they often ruled at the same time in different city–states.

### Sumerian Influence

Sumer was made up of a number of small city–states. Although the political influence of Sumer was weak, the Sumerian culture nevertheless spread throughout the Near East. Sumerian-style statues have been found at Ashur. The city of Mari, which is located in eastern Syria, has strong connections with Mesopotamia. At Ebla, in western Syria, a large cache of clay tablets (approximately 8,000 in total) has been found, inscribed in Sumerian cuneiform writing.

*Detail from a stone wall plaque from Girsu, in present-day Iraq. The seated figure is Ur-Nanshe, ruler of Lagash, one of the Sumerian city-states. The plaque is inscribed in cuneiform and the hole (left) indicates that it might have been mounted on a pole.*

# Nippur

The site of Nippur was occupied for more than 5,000 years until the ninth century CE. Located in present-day Iraq, near the Euphrates River, the city was built on a hill 66 feet (20 m) high and covered more than 750 acres (300 hectares). In the Early Dynastic period, the lands of Sumer and Akkad met at Nippur.

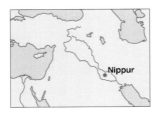

The temple dedicated to Enlil was the most important shrine in Sumer. Enlil, lord of the air, was the chief Sumerian god. The Sumerians believed that the gods met at Nippur to chose the kings of the city-states.

Nippur was never the capital of a dynasty, although kings of the Third Dynasty of Ur may have lived there around 2000 BCE. The rulers of other city-states believed that, because Nippur was so important, whoever controlled it would be entitled to rule all of Sumer and Akkad.

The most significant buildings at Nippur were the ziggurats. These were high temple platforms. On top of the tiers was the temple of Enlil, known as the *ekur* or "mountain house." The first ziggurats were built in the reign of Ur-Nammu (2112–2095 BCE). Enlil's temple was the most important holy place in Mesopotamia. Close to the ziggurat was the temple of Inanna, the goddess of love and war. Today, the remains of the ziggurat are still visible.

*The site of Nippur, including features from a unique scale drawing of the city on a cuneiform tablet dated about 1300 BCE. The tablet shows the temple of Enlil, the city walls, the gates, and the main canal. Thousands of cuneiform tablets have been found at Nippur, where there was a famous scribal school. Excavations at the south end of the site have found where the sharp ends of the wall join.*

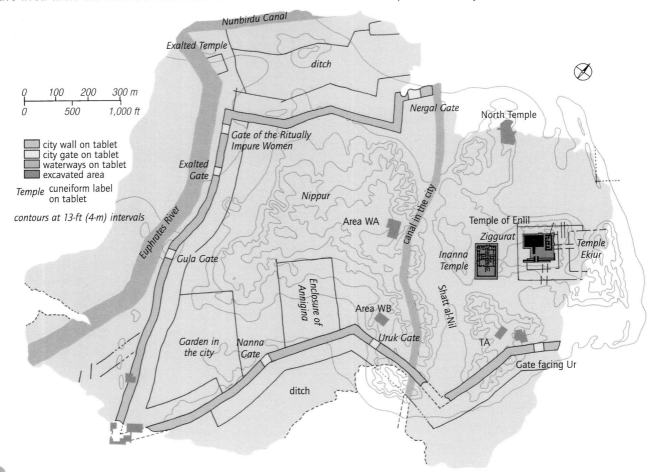

city wall on tablet
city gate on tablet
waterways on tablet
excavated area

*Temple* cuneiform label on tablet

contours at 13-ft (4-m) intervals

Nunbirdu Canal
Exalted Temple
ditch
Nergal Gate
North Temple
Gate of the Ritually Impure Women
Exalted Gate
Nippur
Area WA
Temple of Enlil
Ziggurat
Temple Ekiur
Inanna Temple
Euphrates River
Gula Gate
canal in the city
Enclosure of Annigina
Area WB
Shatt al-Nil
Uruk Gate
TA
Garden in the city
Nanna Gate
ditch
Gate facing Ur

# Ebla

In 1968, archeologists identified Tell Mardikh as the site of the ancient city of Ebla. Tell Mardikh is located in Syria, south of Aleppo. Ebla was inhabited for more than 3,500 years until the start of the ninth century CE. Its cultural peak was between 2500 BCE and 1500 BCE.

One of the most striking finds at Ebla was a library that contained around 8,000 texts recorded on clay tablets. The texts were written in cuneiform, a script created by pressing a wedge-shaped stylus into wet clay. The library was located in "Palace G". Most of the clay tablets were written in Eblaite. This was a local language to Ebla that was previously unknown to archeologists, but which was closely related to the language of Akkad. From the tablets, archaeologists have learned a lot of information about the administration of Ebla. The king was very rich. He owned 80,000 sheep and received an income of 11 pounds (5 kg) of gold and 1,100 pounds (500 kg) of silver every year.

## Ebla and Sumer

Ebla was a rich kingdom. The clay tablets showed that it had many links with Sumer. Some were written in both Eblaite and Sumerian. Fine gold jewelry found in Palace G was made using Sumerian techniques. A limestone inlay was decorated with battle scenes that were like the art of Sumer.

Ebla's peak was between 2400 and 2250 BCE, when the Early Dynastic period ended and Akkadian rulers controlled the city. Ebla had a vast royal complex, and the city's trade routes extended as far as Afghanistan. After a Mesopotamian king, Naram-Sin (2254–2218 BCE), attacked the city, Ebla lost much of its power and thereafter it never recovered its economic wealth and status.

*In this view of the excavations at Ebla, a layer of new bricks has been added to some of the older walls. The picture also shows some stones used to grind flour.*

# Ur

The ancient city of Ur was founded in about 4000 BCE near the Euphrates River. Today, it is located in present-day southern Iraq.

Ur was founded at about the same time as the city of Sumer during the Ubaid period. Some of the oldest remains of Ur were covered by silt from the Euphrates, which helped to preserve them. The silt may have been caused by a huge flood. Certainly, the Bible mentions a large flood in chapters six and eight of *Genesis*.

There are direct references to the city of Ur in the Bible. *Genesis* chapter 11 mentions Ur as being the home of Abraham, the father of the Jewish people. Ur's importance lay in its strategic position. It served as the port from which goods were sent to the Persian Gulf until 1700 BCE. The city was eventually abandoned about 300 BCE. Archeologists think this was probably as a result of more flooding.

The most important buildings in Ur were surrounded by a wall. The main temple was dedicated to the moon god, Nanna, and was built by the kings of the Third Dynasty (2112–2004 BCE). Within the sacred enclosure were the royal tombs.

*BELOW: The remains of the ziggurat at Ur have been reconstructed to give a clear indication of the shape and imposing size of the original structure.*

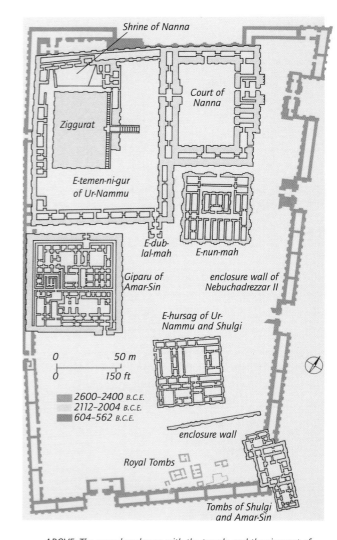

*ABOVE: The sacred enclosure with the temple and the ziggurat of Nanna, the moon god. It was built by the kings of the Third Dynasty of Ur. Ur-Nammu, Shulgi, and Amar-Sin also seem to have lived and been buried here. The royal tombs were inside the walls.*

Lake Van

Lake Urmia

Shubat-Enlil ▲
Tell al-Hawa ▲

Apku ▲

Qatara △
(Tell al-Rimah)

Dur-Sharrukin
(Khorsabad)
▲Nineveh
▲ Arbil
Kalhu

Ashur ● ▲Kar-Tukulti-Ninurta
▲▲▲

*Euphrates*

*Tigris*

Mari ▲

*Ziggurats of Mesopotamia.*
*Ziggurats have been excavated*
*at 16 sites. Others are known*
*from the shape of their mound*
*or from literary sources.*
*Dur-Sharrukin was one of the*
*first to be excavated.*

Dur-Kurigalzu ▲
△ Sippar
Babylon △ Kish
Borsippa △
Nippur ▲
Adab ▲
Uruk ▲ Hamman
▲▲ Larsa
Eridu ▲
Ur

Susa ▲
Deh-i No ▲
Al-Untash-Napirisha
(Choga Zanbil)

▲ Isin city-state, 1900 B.C.E.

**Period of initial ziggurat construction**
▲ Ur III (2100–2000 B.C.E.)
△ Old Babylonian (1900–1700 B.C.E.)
▲ Elamite, Kassite, Middle Assyrian
   (1400–1100 B.C.E.)
▲ Old Babylonian (1900–1700 B.C.E.)

- - - - Ancient coastline
——— Ancient course of river

Scale 1: 8 300 000
0 ————————— 200 km
0 ————————— 150 miles

The
Gulf

## The Royal Cemetery at Ur

During the 1920s, a team of archeologists excavated more than a thousand graves at Ur. They all dated from the end of the Early Dynastic period (2600–2400 BCE), and were notable for their spectacular contents. Within the graves were some amazing treasures. One of the most magnificent finds was an artefact known as the "Standard of Ur." This was a beautiful box decorated with delicate inlay. One side of the box shows a banquet scene, while on the other side there is a depiction of a war procession. Other finds included jewelry made from gold and lapis-lazuli, as well as many gold and silver objects, such as goblets. The discovery of the royal tombs at Ur showed the world the full glory of ancient Sumerian culture

There were inscriptions on some of the graves that identified the burial sites of King Meskalamdug and Queens Puabi and Ninbanda. Archeologists think that the evidence of mass burials proves that human sacrifice took place at Ur. Sometimes kings and queens were buried with their servants. The servants probably died by drinking poison or taking drugs.

# KINGS OF AGADE (2350–2000 BCE)

**When King Sargon** of Akkad conquered both the north and south of the region, Mesopotamia became united for the first time. The Mesopotamians ruled across the Near East, and the Akkadian language was now spoken across the region instead of Sumerian.

## King Sargon of Agade

Sargon was the first king of a new dynasty, the Agade, and he ruled for 56 years. In Akkadian, his name means "the true king," but this hides his true origins. He came from a modest background. According to the Sumerian King List, his father grew dates; according to another record, he was a gardener favored by the goddess Ishtar. Sargon's father became the royal cupbearer at the court of Kish.

Sargon extended his territory by conquering the city–states of Uruk, Ur, Umma, and Lagash in southern Mesopotamia. To demonstrate his power, he built a new capital at Agade, which may have been close to Babylon. He was known as "the King of Kish" and "King of the Land."

## Sargon's Sons

Sargon's sons, Rimush and Manishtushu, continued to expand the empire by fighting against different city–states. The Akkadian empire extended as far north as Ashur and Nineveh and also into the east. The Akkadians also extended their territory as far as Anshan and Sherihum in present-day Iran.

*This stone relief, now in the Louvre in Paris, shows King Sargon I standing next to a tree of life. The king's royal status is shown by his crown and the elaborate style of his hair and beard. Sargon was the founder of the Akkadian dynasty, which was named for the city of Agade.*

## Naram-Sin

Sargon's grandson, Naram-Sin, also had a long reign: 37 years in total. He called himself "King of the Universe." His empire extended from Susa in the east to Ebla, on the Mediterranean coast in the west. He said he was a god and

## KINGS OF AGADE (BCE)

SARGON m. Tashlultum
2334–2279

RIMUSH
2278–2270

MANISHTUSHU
2269–2255

Enheduanna
High priestess at Ur

NARAM-SIN
2254–2218

SHAR-KALI-SHARRI
2217–2193

Emmenanna
High priestess at Ur

## THE THIRD DYNASTY OF UR (BCE)

UR-NAMMU
2112–2095

SHULGI
2094–2047

Ennirgalanna
High priestess at Ur

AMAR-SIN
2046–2038

SHU-SIN
2037–2029

Ennirzianna
High priestess at Ur

IBBI-SIN
2028–2004

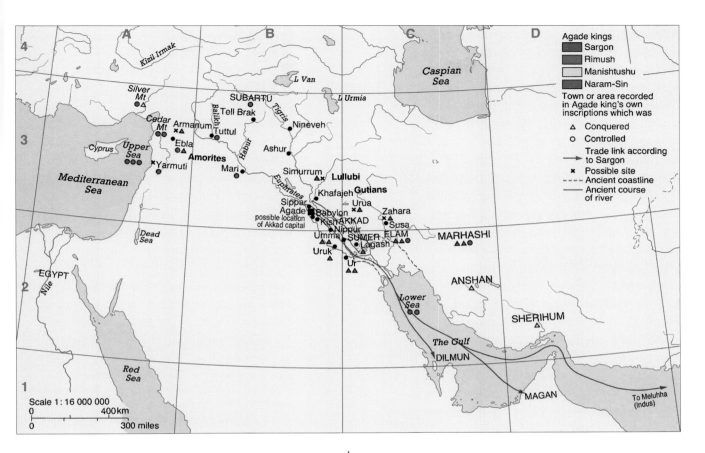

The map contains the following labels:

**Legend (top right):**

Agade kings
- Sargon
- Rimush
- Manishtushu
- Naram-Sin

Town or area recorded in Agade king's own inscriptions which was
- △ Conquered
- ○ Controlled
- → Trade link according to Sargon
- × Possible site
- ---- Ancient coastline
- —— Ancient course of river

**Map labels:**

Kizil Irmak · Silver Mt · SUBARTU · L Van · Caspian Sea · L Urmia · Cedar Mt · Armanum · Tell Brak · Tuttul · Nineveh · Balikh · Tigris · Ebla · Ashur · Habur · Cyprus · Upper Sea · Amorites · Yarmuti · Mari · Simurrum · Lullubi · Mediterranean Sea · Khafajeh · Gutians · Euphrates · Sippar · Urua · Agade · Babylon · Zahara · possible location of Akkad capital · Kish AKKAD · Susa · Dead Sea · Nippur · Umma · SUMER ELAM · MARHASHI · Uruk · Lagash · EGYPT · Nile · Ur · ANSHAN · Lower Sea · SHERIHUM · The Gulf · DILMUN · Red Sea · MAGAN · To Meluhha (Indus)

Scale 1: 16 000 000
0        400km
0        300 miles

made his people call him "god of Agade." Inscriptions on buildings show his name marked with a sign that meant "gods." Naram-Sin's son, Shar-kali-sharri, reigned for 17 years, but the empire of Agade began to collapse because of its internal problems. It also came under attack from the Gutians, who came from the Zagros Mountains. Agade was destroyed: all evidence of its existence disappeared and it has never been found again.

## The Third Dynasty of Ur

With the end of the Akkadian empire, the Sumerians took control in the region once again. King Ur-Nammu built a ziggurat, temples, and a palace at Ur. King Ur-Nammu's power base was in southern Mesopotamia. When one of his sons married a daughter of the king of Mari, the two nations were linked. Ur-Nammu's son, Shulgi, ruled for 47 years.

*The kings of Agade conquered an empire that stretched from the Mediterranean to modern-day Iran. Sargon claimed that he ruled the whole world "from the sunrise to the sunset." This boast could have been a later tradition. From their widespread territories, the kings of Agade obtained such raw materials as wood from Lebanon and silver from Anatolia.*

He also claimed to be a descendant of the gods. To emphasize his power, Shulgi carried on the building program started by his father. He defeated other city–states and expanded his empire to the east and to the north.

Shulgi also carried out large-scale reforms, including making the governors ("ensis") and military commanders ("shagins") report directly to him. He took over temple lands, introduced a new calendar, reorganized the system of weights, established a code of law, and brought in new taxes. Animals rather than money were used to pay taxes. In one year, 28,000 cattle and 350,000 sheep were paid in taxes.

# RIVAL KINGDOMS (2000–1600 BCE)

**Around 2000 BCE,** Mesopotamia was no longer united. The Third Dynasty of Ur broke up into a number of smaller kingdoms, of which the most important were Isin and Larsa. This period is named after these two kingdoms. King Rim-sin of Larsa was the most famous of all the kings of this period. He ruled from 1822 to 1763 BCE. In 1804 BCE, he conquered Ur and then, 10 years later, Isin.

New peoples arrived in Mesopotamia. The Amorites, who were nomads from the desert regions of Arabia and who spoke a Semitic language, settled among the Akkadian and Sumerian peoples. The Amorites became increasingly powerful in the kingdoms of Babylon, Kish, and Larsa. Another group of new arrivals were the Hurrians. They came from Anatolia and spoke an Indo-European language. They settled in northern Mesopotamia and western Syria. We know this because written texts from Alalakh, on the Orontes River in Syria, show that nearly half of the population had Hurrian names.

## Trade in the South

Trade was widespread among the southern Mesopotamian kingdoms. They exported silver, oils, textiles, and barley to the Gulf region and to more remote kingdoms. Imports included such commodities as copper, gold, ivory, lapis lazuli, and pearls. Copper came from Magan (present-day Oman), while beads found at Mesopotamian sites show that the region had links with the Harappan culture of the Indus Valley (modern-day Pakistan). Many of the goods were shipped through the region of Dilmun (probably present-day Bahrain).

## Trade and Conquest in the North

The kingdoms of northern Mesopotamia also traded with other city–states. One settlement, Ashur, on the Tigris River was an important

*A donkey caravan at the "karum" (merchant suburb) outside Kanesh, an important trade center in Anatolia. Donkeys have arrived from Ashur, bringing textiles and tin from Iran. Other donkeys are being loaded to continue farther west. One of the merchants is watching his scribe count the goods.*

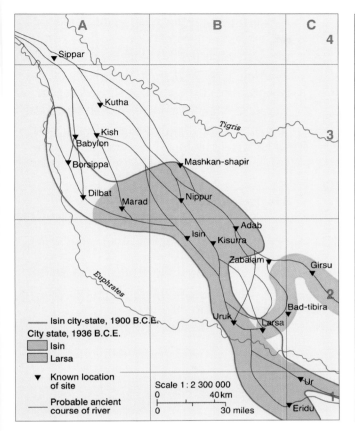

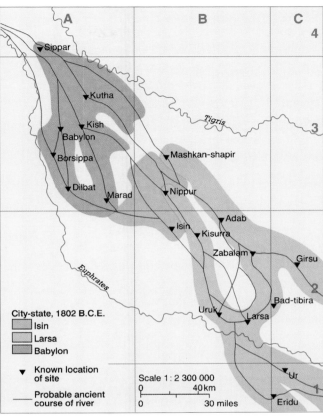

*City-states of the Isin and Larsa period. The rival states that followed the Third Dynasty of Ur were often at war with each other. In 1936 BCE (left), Isin was the largest. Twenty-six years later, in 1910 BCE, it included only Nippur. The cities of Ur and Eridu were still ruled by Larsa in 1802 BCE (right), while, in the north, Babylon had become a major kingdom.*

trade center, where merchants traded in wool, textiles, and tin. The tin was used to make bronze, which, in turn, was used in the manufacture weapons and other goods. It was originally mined in Afghanistan and Iran and then brought to Ashur by donkey caravans to Kanesh in central Turkey.

Throughout the period of his reign, the Amorite leader, Shamshi-Adad, defeated many of the northern kingdoms, including Ashur. His kingdom stretched from the Zagros Mountains to Mari, on the Euphrates River (now in Syria). He was a strong ruler and kept the Amorite Empire together. However, on his death, his two sons could not keep control of the vast territory and the empire began to fall apart. During this time, some of the old kingdoms were restored. In Mari, Zimri-Lim retook his throne until 1757 BCE, when he was overthrown by the king of Babylon, Hammurabi.

### KINGDOMS OF MESOPOTAMIA (2025–1595 BCE)

**First Dynasty of Isin, (2017–1794 BCE)**
Isme-Dagan (1953-1935 BCE)
Lipit-Ishtar (1934-1924 BCE)

**Larsa Dynasty (2025-1763 BCE)**
Rim-Sin I (1822-1763 BCE)

**1763 BCE**
Rim Sin I defeated by Hammurabi, ends the Larsa Dynasty

**First Dynasty of Babylon (1894-1595 BCE)**
Hammurabi (1792-1750 BCE)
Lipit-Ishtar (1934-1924 BCE)

**Asur**
Shamshi-Adad I (c.1813-1781 BCE)
Ishme-Dagan I (1780-1741 BCE)

**Mari**
Zimri-Lim (1779-1757 BCE)

**1757 BCE**
Hammurabi defeats Zimri-Lim, kingdom of Mari ends

# LAW AND SOCIETY

**Justice was a** very important part of the Mesopotamian way of life. Its kings wanted to rule wisely and justly. King Ur-Nammu of Ur (2112–2095 BCE) wrote what is thought to be the first known law code in the world. His son, Shulgi of Ur, also created a code, as did other rulers, such as Lipit-Ishtar of Isin and Dadusha of Eshnunna. The most famous code to survive was written by King Hammurabi of Babylon, who ruled from 1792 to 1750 BCE.

## Hammurabi's Law Code

The law code was carved on to a basalt stele or tablet, 90 inches (3.5 m) tall. Hammurabi set out his beliefs in the opening words: "To cause justice to prevail in the land, to destroy the wicked and the evil, that the strong may not oppress the weak."

Hammurabi's law code contained 282 sections that covered many different areas, including property law and commercial law. If one person committed a crime against another, they were expected to pay for their crime with a fine, in the form of silver. This was a custom inherited from the Sumerians. The concept of punishment found in the Bible's Old Testament, "Life for life, eye for eye, tooth for tooth, hand for hand, foot for foot" (Deuteronomy, chapter 19, verse 21) is also found in Hammurabi's code.

## Babylonian Society

According to Hammurabi's law code, Babylonian society divided into three social classes. These were *awilum* (the Akkadian word that means "man"), *mushkenum*, and *wardum*. The awilum were "freemen," who may have owned land. The freemen may have had to serve in the military,

*This is a detail of regulations from the law code of Hammurabi, inscribed in cuneiform script on a basalt stele from Babylon in about 1760 BCE.*

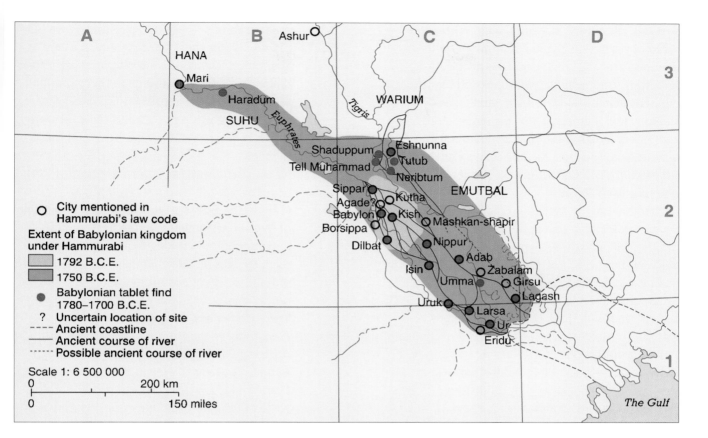

Map labels (clockwise): A, B, Ashur, C, D, HANA, Mari, 3, Haradum, WARIUM, Tigris, SUHU, Euphrates, Shaduppum, Eshnunna, Tell Muhammad, Tutub, Neribtum, Sippar, Kutha, EMUTBAL, Agade?, Babylon, Kish, 2, Borsippa, Mashkan-shapir, Dilbat, Nippur, Adab, Isin, Zabalam, Umma, Girsu, Uruk, Lagash, Larsa, Ur, Eridu, 1, The Gulf

Legend:
○ City mentioned in Hammurabi's law code
Extent of Babylonian kingdom under Hammurabi
  1792 B.C.E.
  1750 B.C.E.
● Babylonian tablet find 1780–1700 B.C.E.
? Uncertain location of site
- - - Ancient coastline
—— Ancient course of river
······ Possible ancient course of river

Scale 1: 6 500 000
0          200 km
0                150 miles

*Hammurabi's kingdom. Hammurabi ruled over Mesopotamia only in the second part of his reign (1792–1750 BCE). He captured Isin and Uruk in 1787 BCE. Later, in 1763 BCE, with the help of the kings of Mari and Eshnunna, he conquered Rim-Sin I of Larsa. In 1761 BCE Hammurabi defeated Mari and in 1755 BCE he was victorious over Eshnunna.*

and pay taxes. The mushkenum could speak in the assembly of freemen, but probably did not own property. The wardum was the slave class.

If an awilum could not pay his taxes to the king or if he got himself into debt, he could sell himself, his wife, or his children as slaves. When an awilum died, his property was divided up between his sons.

The king used slaves to build roads, to dig canals, and to do other task for the community. Slaves were expensive to buy, so few people owned them. Most farms were farmed by tenant farmers who had to give some of their harvest to the landowner in return for food, animals, and other things they needed.

## Penalties Under Hammurabi's Code

Under Hammurabi's code of law, there were different punishments for the same crime. The punishment that would be meted out depended on the victim's social class. If an awilum was the victim, the punishment was retributive (that is, the same action was carried out on the person responsible). Law 196 of the code says: "If an awilum has put out the eye of a mar-awilum (the son of an awilum), they shall put out his eye."

If the victim was from the other social classes, then money was paid instead. Law 198 says: "If an awilum has put out the eye of a mushkenum or broken his bone, he shall pay one mina of silver."

The notion of an "eye for an eye," or the justice of retribution, was probably introduced to Mesopotamia by the Amorites, because there is no evidence of it in Sumerian law.

# MITTANI AND THE ASSYRIANS

**Around 1500 BCE,** the kingdom of Mittani established itself as the major power in northern Mesopotamia and the Levant. The people of Mittani were Hurrians, who spoke a language different from other West Asian languages. The Hurrians had Indo-European customs, such as worshiping Indian gods. They also had a powerful new weapon, the horse-drawn chariot.

## Warfare with Egypt

Under Ahmose, the founder of the 18th Dynasty, Egypt was a united and powerful force. During the New Kingdom, the Egyptians had conquered much of the Levant and Palestine, inflicting great damage. Amenophis II (1427–1401 BCE) led an army into Mittani territory. He took the city of Qadesh on the Orontes River.

## The Amarna Letters

We only know about the life of the Mittanians from foreign accounts, as they did not leave any written records themselves. They are mentioned in Egyptian records known as the

*This carving from the wall of a tomb at Abu Simbel, Egypt, from the 14th–13th centuries BCE shows Hittite soldiers in battle.*

Amarna Letters. These 350 clay tablets are full of information about the government of the Egyptian New Kingdom's territories. They record diplomatic dealings between the pharaohs and several independent countries, including Mittani.

Marriage was often used to cement relations between different states. The harems of the pharaohs often included foreign princesses. Negotiating royal marriages was often complicated. The pharaoh Tuthmosis IV (1401–1391 BCE) had to ask Artatama, the king of Mittani, seven times for the hand of his daughter before the king finally agreed. The marriage was probably intended to stop the growing power of the Hittites and the Assyrians.

## The Hittites and Assyrians

The capital of the Hittites was Hattusas in Anatolia. The Hittites contended for control of Mittani. They ended Hammurabi's dynasty when Mursilis I (1626–1595 BCE) took over Babylon. The Hittites maintained peaceful relations with the Egyptian pharaohs. Suppiluliumas I, their king, formed an alliance with the Assyrians and married his daughter to the king of Babylon.

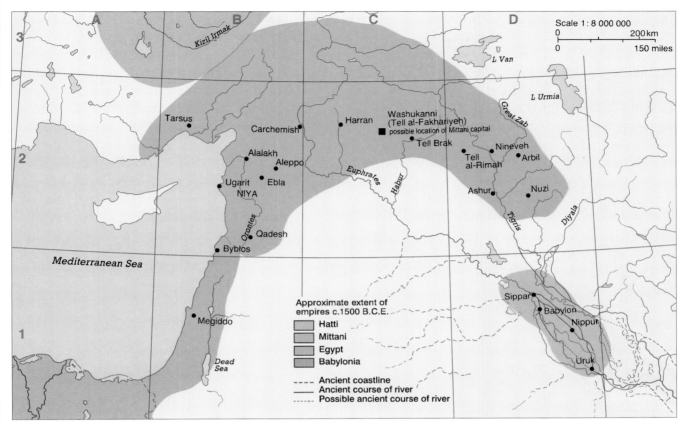

The empire of Mittani in about 1500 BCE. The empire stretched east from Assyria to the Levant. Washukanni, the capital city, has not been positively identified, but may be Tell al-Fakhariyeh in northern Syria. The region around the upper part of the Habur River was the heartland of the empire. Mittanian documents have also been found nearby at Tell Brak.

He won battles in Anatolia, the Levant, and northern Mesopotamia, thereby reducing the lands held by Mittani, which had by this time grown weaker.

The Assyrian king Adad-nirari (1305–1274 BCE) captured Washukanni and made its ruler subject to the Adad-nirari. The Mittanian kingdom ended when Adad-nirari's son, Shalmaneser I (1273–1244 BCE) annexed it. This left the Assyrians and the Hittites as the most powerful people in Mesopotamia.

This is one of the 350 clay tablets known as the Amarna Letters for their discovery at Tell Amarna in central Egypt. The tablets record the diplomatic affairs of the pharaohs Amenophis III and Akhenaten in Akkadian, the international language of the time.

# THE KASSITES (1600–1200 BCE)

**The Kassites ruled** Babylon for four centuries after the Hittite conquest of the city in 1595 BCE. The Kassites ruled from the late 15th to the 12th century BCE. According to the Babylonian King List, the city had 36 Kassite kings. The origins of the Kassites are unclear, but they may have come from Central Asia. They did not speak a Semitic language, and to date only 48 Kassite words have been identified. The Kassites were famous horsemen and some of the words are technical terms for horses. When the Kassites first arrived in the city of Babylon, they seem to have been agricultural workers. Even later on, at the time when their kings ruled over Babylon, the Kassites do not appear to have been a large group.

## Dur-Kurigalzu

The Kassites rebuilt temples at Ur, Uruk, and Isin. The best-preserved example of Kassite work is the site of Agar Quf, known as Dur-Kurigalzu, located close to present-day Baghdad. The city was built to defend against attacks from Assyria and Elam. As well as a palace, the Kassites built a ziggurat, 188 feet (58 m) high. Although Dur-Kurigalzu was a big city, the Kassites considered Babylon to be the capital of their empire.

## Kassite Art and Culture

The Kassites wrote thousands of documents on tablets and their artists drew realistic pictures, particularly of animals. The Kassites were the first people of West Asia to make molded baked

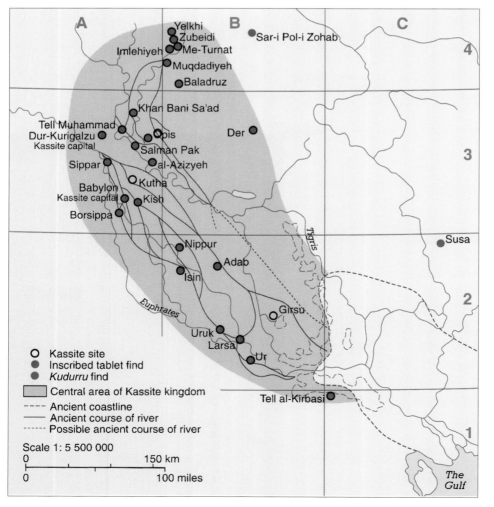

The Kassite kingdom in the 13th century BCE. This was an empire that covered most of southern Mesopotamia. It bordered Elam in the east, (now modern-day Iran) and the Assyrian territories in the north. The Elamites overran the Kassite kingdom in the mid-12th century BCE. They took back some of the war booty from Babylon, including Hammurabi's law-code stele and Naram-Sin's victory stele, to their capital city, Susa. The booty was discovered there in the 19th century by the members of a French expedition.

## The Kassite Dynasty c.1570–1154 BCE

*Selected Kassite kings. (Other rulers from the same period shown in brackets.)*

c.1570 BCE Agum II

c.1510 BCE Burna-Buriash I

c.1390 BCE Kurigalzu I (Amenophis III of Egypt)

1359–1333 BCE Burna-Buriash II

1332–1308 BCE Kurigalzu II (Akhenaten of Egypt)

1263–1255 BCE Kadashman-Enlil II (Hattusilis III, Hittites)

1232–1225 BCE Kashtiliash IV (Assyrian king Tukulti-Ninurta sacks Babylon

1170–1158 BCE Marduk-apla-iddina

1156–1154 BCE Enlil-nadin-ahi

## Kassite Kings (BCE)

| Kara-indash | c.1415 |
| --- | --- |
| Kadashman-Harbe I | |
| Kurigalzu I | |
| Kadashman-Enlil I | 1374–1360 |
| Burna-Buriash II | 1359–1333 |
| Kara-hardash | 1333 |
| Nazi-bugash | 1333 |
| Kurigalzu II | 1332–1308 |
| Nazi-maruttash | 1307–1282 |
| Kadashman-Turgu | 1281–1264 |
| Kadashman-Enlil II | 1263–1255 |
| Kudur-Enlil | 1254–1246 |
| Shagarakti-shuriash | 1245–1233 |
| Kashtiliash IV | 1232–1225 |
| Tulkulli-Ninurta | 1224–1216 |
| Enlil-nadin-shumi | 1224 |
| Kadashman-Harbe II | 1223–1222 |
| Adad-shuma-iddina | 1221–1216 |
| Adad-shuma-usur | 1215–1186 |
| Melishipak | 1185–1171 |
| Marduk-apla-iddina I | 1170–1158 |
| Zababa-shuma-iddina | 1157 |
| Enlil-nadin-ahi | 1156–1154 |

bricks used to make decorative wall friezes. Such bricks were still being used a thousand years later in the palaces built by Darius at Susa and Nebuchadrezzar at Babylon. The Inanna Temple at Uruk shows gods in human form on the outer wall. The Kassites were also skillful stone carvers. They carved boundary stones ("kudurru") with highly decorated images of beasts, symbolizing gods who were believed to witness the giving of land by royal decree that was then marked by the boundary stones.

## Kassite Kings

The Amarna Letters mention several Kassite kings. One king, Burna-Buriash II (1359–1333 BCE) complained that the Egyptian delegation sent to collect his daughter for her wedding did not show enough respect as they only sent five carriages. The letters also list the many gifts that were exchanged between the Kassite king and the Egyptian pharaoh.

However, the most famous Kassite king was Kurigalzu II (1332–1308 BCE). He was a great military leader. He attacked the Elamites and took Susa, their capital. Later, the Elamites attacked the Kassites. Babylon was destroyed, and the Kassite period ended in 1154 BCE.

# NEW POWERS

**About 1200 BCE,** the Hittite empire came under attack from raiders who appeared in the Near East and the Levant. They also threatened Egypt. For the next thousand years, the political makeup of the Near East was very different.

## The Sea Peoples

These seafaring raiders, known as the "Sea Peoples," were probably made up of different ethnic groups, and may have come from the Aegean Sea in the west. When they attacked Egypt and the Levant, Pharaoh Ramesses III (1194–1163 BCE) successfully defeated them.

One of the tribes driven out of Egypt by Ramesses III settled on the Mediterranean coastal plains. In the Bible, these people were called the Philistines, from which the word

"Palestine" comes. The Philistines adopted the local Canaanite culture, but their ties to the Aegean can be seen in their pottery which shows Mycenaean (Greek) influence.

## Babylon and Assyria

Babylon's power grew again for a brief period under Nebuchadrezzar I (1126–1105 BCE). He attacked neighboring Susa and brought back booty, including the statue of Marduk that had been taken from Babylon by the Elamite king, Shutruk-Nahhunte in 1159 BCE.

Assyria became a great power when King Tiglath-Pileser I (1115–1077 BCE) increased his

*The Assyrian empire of Tiglath-Pileser I. The empire extended to the western Euphrates and was not troubled by the Sea Peoples, who overran Egypt, the Levant, and Anatolia.*

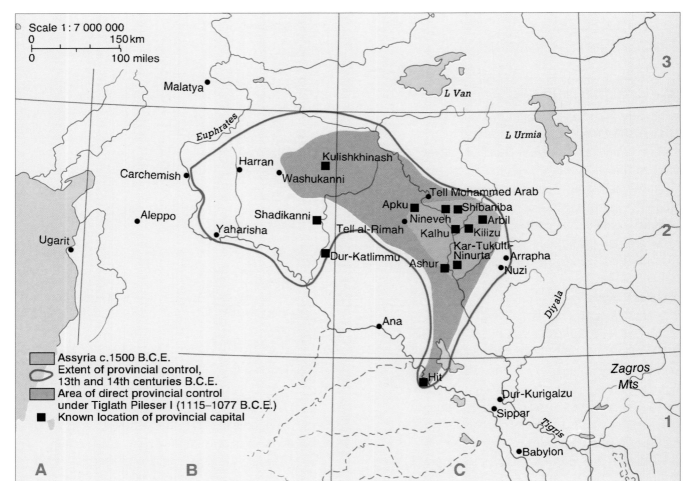

Scale 1 : 7 000 000

Assyria c.1500 B.C.E.
Extent of provincial control, 13th and 14th centuries B.C.E.
Area of direct provincial control under Tiglath Pileser I (1115–1077 B.C.E.)
■ Known location of provincial capital

## The Aramaeans

The Aramaeans were nomads who came from the Syrian Desert. They blocked the Assyrians from the Mediterranean by establishing small kingdoms in northern Syria and the Levant. The power of the Aramaeans grew and Adad-apla-iddina (1069–1048 BCE), king of Babylon, was known as the "Aramaean usurper." The Aramaeans spoke Aramaic. This language replaced Akkadian as the main language of the Near East until Arabic emerged in 700 CE. Some of their letters survive today in the modern Armenian and Georgian alphabets.

territories as far as the Levant. We know about his battles against peoples like the Ahlamu and Aramaeans because they were recorded in stone carvings at his palace in Nineveh. Some of the war scenes are very shocking.

*The infantry troops of Tiglath-Pileser I (1115–1077 BCE) lay siege to a city in Syria. Its gates are firmly shut, but its walls are being breached by a movable wooden siege-engine that is manned from the inside and carries archers on the top.*

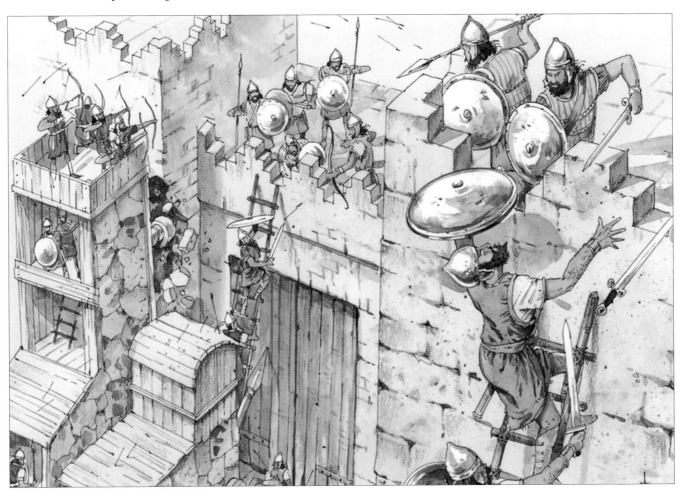

# ISRAEL AND JUDAH

**"Israel is laid waste"** proclaimed the inscriptions on the victory stele of Pharaoh Merneptah in 1229 BCE. This was not a reference to the country of Israel, which did not then exist, but to a people who had recently appeared in West Asia.

## The Bible and Israelite History

The Bible records how the Israelites came to settle in the land of Canaan. Accounts of their departure from Egypt and of the wanderings of the 12 tribes around the Sinai Peninsula in search of a home are included in the book of Exodus. The books of Joshua and Judges then tell the story of how the Israelites tried to settle in Canaan. They were repelled by the local people and the Philistines who were living on the coastal plain.

Around 1080 BCE, the Philistines tried to expand from their rich coastal base into the hills where the Israelite tribes had settled. To fight the Philistines, the Israelite tribes united together under Saul, the first king of Israel. The two books of Samuel recount how the Israelite monarchy developed.

## King David

King David was one of the greatest kings of the Israelites, although he was initially installed as a vassal (puppet king) by the Philistines at Hebron

*Solomon's Temple in Jerusalem. The plan of the building resembled Phoenician architecture. It was rectangular, with a porch flanked by a pair of bronze columns called Jachin and Boaz. The Holy Place was paneled in cedar wood. Only the high priest could enter the Holy of Holies through its double doors. In the temple forecourt, stood a huge bronze basin filled with water. It was supported by 12 bronze bulls. This basin was used for rituals.*

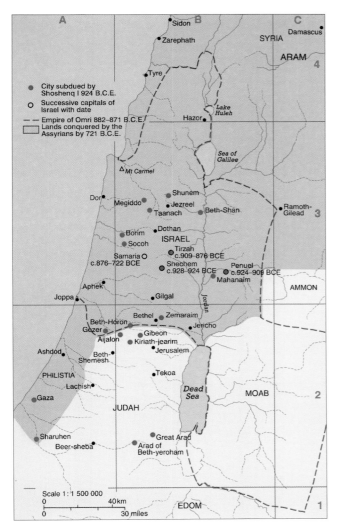

*The united kingdom of Israel and Judah. Jerusalem was made the capital city by King David and made splendid by his son, King Solomon. When Solomon died, the kingdom divided into Israel in the north and Judah in the south. In 924 BCE, the Egyptian pharaoh Shoshenq invaded, but the two kingdoms survived intact until the late eighth century BCE.*

city. David brought the Ark of Covenant (the sacred container of the scrolls of Jewish law) to Jerusalem. The Philistines had captured it earlier.

### Solomon's Achievements

King Solomon was the son of King David. He added to the splendor of Jerusalem. He built the Temple of Jerusalem to house the Ark of Covenant. The temple walls were said to be lined with cedar wood and the floors to be made of fir-wood overlaid with gold. Today, the Muslim Dome of the Rock stands on the site. Archeologists have not been able to find any remains of Solomon's Temple, but there are descriptions of it in the Bible.

King Solomon also built a splendid palace from luxury materials such as ivory and beams carved from the finest cedar and cypress wood. The Phoenician style, which was known for its sophistication, influenced the design of his palace. The Phoenicians lived to the north of the kingdom of Israel and Judah.

Sites outside Jerusalem have yielded more archeological confirmation of King Solomon's ambitious building program. He built triple-chambered city gates, remains of which have been found at Megiddo, Hazor, and Gezer. He also built stables for hundreds of horses at Megiddo, because his army used horse-drawn chariots. At Ezion-Gezer on the Gulf of Aqaba, Solomon had industrial buildings erected to smelt copper. He also built a fleet of ships in order to trade along the Red Sea with east Africa and Arabia.

in Judah. Hebron later became the first capital of King David's kingdom. In 995 BCE, David overcame the Philistines and took Jerusalem. Jerusalem was then the capital of the Jebusites, who were a Canaanite tribe.

Jerusalem was well located and King David used it as a base from which to control Judah in the south and Israel in the north. David also established Jerusalem as the religious heart of the Israelite nation and designated it a royal

# Kalhu (Nimrud)

The city of Kalhu, also known as Nimrud, is located in present-day northern Iraq, where the Tigris and Great Zab rivers meet, south of the city of Mosul. Kalhu's importance dates from the time when king Ashurnasirpal II (883–859 BCE) selected it as his capital city. Shalmaneser III (858–824 BCE) built a palace there. In the book of Genesis in the Bible, Kalhu is mentioned as the city of Calah.

## Ashurnasirpal's City

After Ashurnasirpal II moved his capital from Ashur to Kalhu by 878 BCE, he embarked on a massive building program. In order to supply water to the city, a canal was dug from the Great Zab River. Ashurnasirpal II enclosed the city with massive walls. These walls were 5 miles (8 km) long and 70 million bricks were used in their construction. The city covered 900 acres (360 hectares) and included a ziggurat and temples, as well as a splendid palace.

The king was proud of his new capital city. An inscription records that Ashurnasirpal II held a magnificent feast or banquet to celebrate the completion of the Northwest Palace. The feast lasted 10 days and was attended by 69,574 guests from all over the Assyrian empire.

*The Northwest Palace at Kalhu. Around the outer courtyard were offices. The throne room was used for official functions. The king's private quarters were around the inner courtyard.*

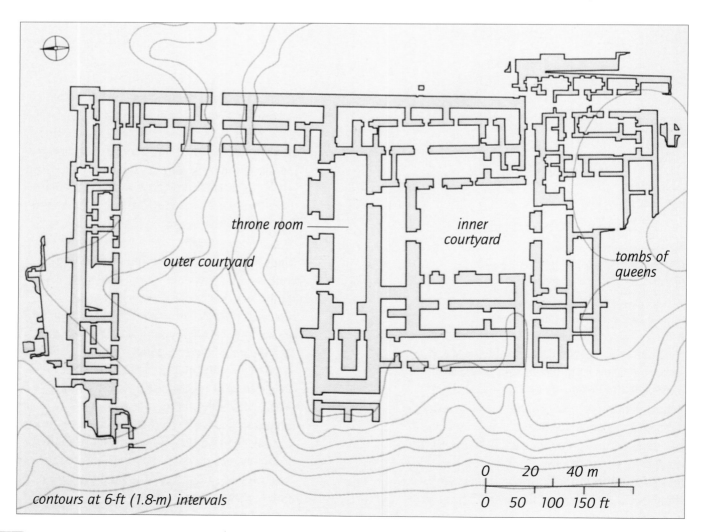

throne room

inner courtyard

outer courtyard

tombs of queens

contours at 6-ft (1.8-m) intervals

0    20    40 m

0    50    100   150 ft

*RIGHT: The Balawat gates, a pair of massive bronze-clad gates built by Shalmaneser III, were found 10 miles (16 km) northeast of Kalhu. The detail (above) shows chariots with six-spoked wheels, typical of the ninth century BCE. Each leaf of the gates was about 6.5 feet (2 m) wide and 13 feet (4 m) high. Sixteen embossed bands of bronze were engraved with scenes from Shalmaneser's conquests, including campaigns against the Urartu, who lived in the Lake Van region of present-day Turkey.*

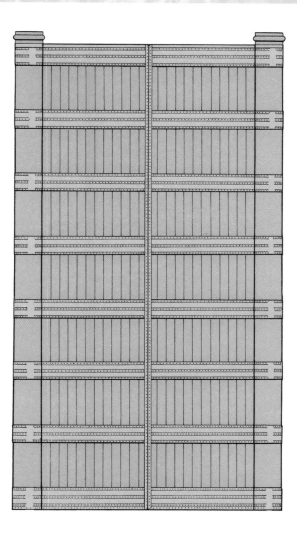

## Kalhu's Sculptures

Archeologists made some spectacular discoveries during the excavations at Kalhu. In particular, they found a number of carved stone panels that originally decorated the courtyard walls and the adjacent throne room of the Northwest Palace. The detailed carved panels show the king at war, going hunting, and also fulfilling his religious duties. In one scene, Ashurnasirpal is shown shooting an arrow at a lion from a chariot. The panels also depict the king receiving gifts from foreign visitors. One of the gifts the king receives is a monkey. The reliefs were once brightly painted and they show the fabrics, clothes, and jewelry that the king and his officials wore.

## Treasures of Kalhu

Kings and courtiers were buried in tombs that contained vaulted chambers. When three royal tombs were excavated at Kalhu, they were discovered with their contents intact. Grave objects that were found included gold jewelry that was in perfect condition.

Another fabulous discovery was made in a well and in the arsenal at Fort Shalmaneser. Several thousands of pieces of carved ivory were found in the well. It is thought that many of the pieces were part of the war booty collected by the Assyrians when they fought in the Levant. They were most likely hidden in the well to protect them when the Medes took Kalhu in 612 BCE.

**The Assyrian empire** thrived between 750 and 626 BCE because of a number of strong rulers who took it to the peak of its power.

## Tiglath-Pileser III

Tiglath-Pileser III (744–727 BCE) was a powerful and successful leader. He undertook a number of reforms that helped strengthen the Assyrian empire. He reorganized the army and instead of having vassal rulers he installed loyal provincial governors. He linked the various parts of his empire by a "royal mail" service. Messengers traveled in mule-drawn chariots to every corner of the empire. To control his empire, Tiglath-Pileser III expelled many of the people he conquered to prevent future uprisings.

*A royal procession enters Babylon through the Ishtar gate. The gate was more than 46 feet (14 m) high and made of blue-glazed bricks that were decorated with bulls and dragons. The king rides in his chariot, sheltered by an umbrella, the symbol of royalty. The first chariot carries his senior court official.*

Shalmaneser V (726–722 BCE) followed his father. He only reigned for a short period and may have been killed during the three-year siege of Samaria. We only know about his reign from a mention in the Bible.

## Sargon II

Sargon II (722–705 BCE) was an efficient and capable leader, although how he came to power remains unclear. He established Assyrian rule as

### KINGS OF ASSYRIA 744–626 BCE

**744–727 BCE** Tiglath-Pileser III

**726–722 BCE** Shalmaneser V

**722–705 BCE** Sargon II

**704–681 BCE** Sennacherib

**680–669 BCE** Esarhaddon

**668–626 BCE** Ashurbanipal

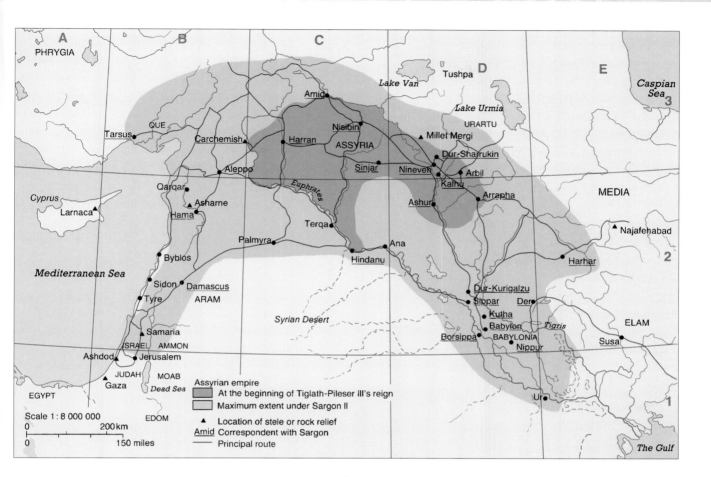

The Assyrian empire in the late eighth century BCE. The capital city of the empire was Ashur in northern Mesopotamia. The lands controlled by the Assyrians extended from Ur near the Gulf and included the kingdom of Israel. Jerusalem and the kingdom of Judah only came under their control between 733 and 650 BCE. An efficient road system linked the distant parts of the empire, with travelers' rest-houses at regular intervals along the highways.

far west as Egypt by defeating an alliance of Syrian states at Qarqar on the Orontes River. Other notable victories included defeating the Phrygians, whose ruler was the legendary King Midas. Sargon II destroyed the capital of the Urartu, Musasir, in 714 BCE and obliged the kings of Cyprus to pay tribute to him. In 709 BCE, Sargon II became king of Babylon. His empire now stretched from the Gulf to the Sinai desert. Sargon died in battle in 705 BCE, however. His body was never recovered, so he could not be buried in his palace.

## Sargon's Successors

Sargon's son was named Sennacherib (704–681 BCE). Some of his achievements are recorded in the Bible, including his capture of Lachish in 701 BCE and his dealings with Hezekiah, who was the king of Judah. Sennacherib destroyed the city of Babylon in 694 BCE. One of his sons then murdered him. Esarhaddon (680–669 BCE), the crown prince, claimed the throne and expanded the empire with the capture of Memphis from the Egyptians in 671 BCE. He died at battle in 669 BCE.

Esarhaddon's two sons succeeded him. Ashurbanipal was the king of Assyria and was a better military leader and scholar than his brother, the king of Babylon. Ashurbanipal is known to have collected many cuneiform texts from all over his empire which he kept in his famous library at Nineveh.

# Ashur

**The site of** Ashur is a rocky outcrop of land overlooking the River Tigris in northern Iraq. It was occupied as early as 2300 BCE as Sumerian- style statues, dating from the Early Dynastic period, found at the site testify.

Ashur was located on an important trade route to Anatolia. In 2000 BCE, merchants established a trading colony at Kanesh in Anatolia to trade with Ashur. Donkey caravans carried textiles, as well as tin mined in Iran, to Ashur. From there, goods were transported to other cities of the empire. We know about the trade between Ashur and Kanesh because of the cuneiform tablets found at Kanesh.

## Assyrian Capital

Ashur's location made it ideal as a trade center, but it was not the obvious choice for the capital of the Assyrian empire because there was little farmland around it. Nevertheless, the Middle and Late Assyrian kings chose it as their capital. The tombs of five Assyrian kings have been found at Ashur. Adad-nirari I (1305–1274 BCE) built a large palace and Tukulti-Ninurta I (1243–1207 BCE) constructed a defensive moat around the city. He also rebuilt a temple and started work on another palace.

Even though Ashurnasirpal II (833–859 BCE) moved the capital to Kalhu, the city of Ashur continued to be the religious capital. As well as a ziggurat, there were many temples at Ashur. Later kings continued to construct religious buildings, including three ziggurats and at least 38 temples inside the large city.

Ashur was looted between 614 and 612 BCE, when the Medes from Iran invaded Assyria. In the second and first centuries BCE, the city was occupied again and renamed Labbana.

*The site of Ashur. There were many temples, including the temple of the city god, also called Ashur. The palace, ziggurat, and temples were sited on the steep northern cliffs overlooking the old course of the River Tigris. The river now flows on the eastern side of the promontory. The western side was protected by a wall and a moat.*

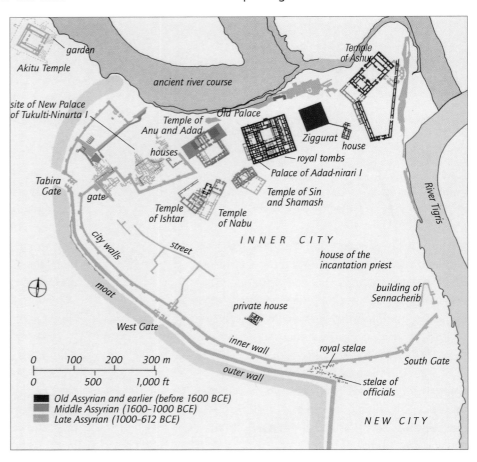

# Nineveh

*This detail of an alabaster low-relief frieze found at Nineveh, created in about 695 BCE, shows part of a buffalo hunt. As in other West Asian cultures, hunting played an important part in society as a display of prowess and social status.*

Nineveh was famed as one of the most magnificent cities in Mesopotamia. It is located on the east side of the Tigris River, close to Mosul in northern Iraq. It,like Ashur, occupied a strategically important site for trading, because it stood on one of the main western trade routes to the Mediterranean. Originally, the city was surrounded by more than 7 miles (12 km) of city walls. The city contained two principal mounds: Nebi Yunus (the citadel); and Kuyunjik (the arsenal).

## City of Treasures

King Manishtushu (2269–2255 BCE) founded the temple of Ishtar at Nineveh. Its fame was widespread and Hammurabi mentioned it in his law code. One of the greatest Mesopotamian art treasures, a bronze life-sized head of Naram-Sin (2254–2218 BCE), was found here.

A Late Assyrian ruler, Sennacherib (705–681 BCE), made Nineveh his capital. He built the Southwest palace that was lavishly decorated with carved stone reliefs. These showed many scenes, including the siege and capture of Lachish. Sennacherib's grandson, Ashurbanipal (669–627 BCE), built the North Palace to store his cuneiform library.

Nineveh is mentioned in the Bible and its downfall was prophesied. In 612 BCE, the Babylonians and Medes attacked and destroyed Nineveh. Its fall marked the collapse of the Assyrian Empire.

**Between 900 and** 681 BCE, the city of Babylon struggled to find stability and to prosper. Twenty-four kings ruled during this period. Its fortunes improved when Esarhaddon (680–669 BCE) became king. Over the next century, the city flourished to become rich and powerful and known across the Ancient World.

## Nabopolassar

Nabopolassar (625–605 BCE) came from nowhere to found the New Babylonian or Neo-Babylonian dynasty. He claimed to be the "son of nobody," who had fought the Assyrians for 10 years in Babylonian territories. He gained enough power to move north to attack Ashur, the religious capital of the Assyrians.

Before Nabopolassar could attack Ashur, the Medes from northwest Iran looted the city. The Babylonian and Median armies joined forces to capture Nineveh in 612 BCE and extensively looted the city. In 1990, archeologists discovered skeletons at one of the city's gates. Their bones were muddled together, suggesting that they had been killed while trying to flee the city.

## Nebuchadrezzar

Nebuchadrezzar was the son of Nabopolassar. Before he became king, Nebuchadrezzar had already defeated the Egyptian pharaoh Necho in 605 BCE at Carchemish in Syria. He did not attack Judah because King Jehoiakim paid him tribute. After his father died in 605 BCE, Nebuchadrezzar returned to Babylon to be crowned king. To get back for his coronation, he walked 30 miles (48 km) a day for three weeks.

## Babylon and the Jews

King Josiah's son, Jehoiakim (609–598 BCE), succeeded his father as king of Judah and initially accepted Nebuchadrezzar as his superior. Then, around 600 BCE, he rebelled. Nebuchadrezzar went to war with Judah and took Jerusalem in 597 BCE. He captured the royal family, including the new king, Jehoiakim's son Jehoiachin, his mother, wives, and officials. They were taken to Babylon in chains.

Nebuchadrezzar then installed Jehoiachin's uncle, Zedekiah (597–587 BCE) to be king of Judah, but he rebelled as well. The Babylonians besieged Jerusalem and broke through its defenses in 587–586 BCE. They looted the city, destroying much of it and expelling the Jewish population, many of whom were sent to Babylon. They also removed treasures from the Temple. The Bible records these events.

## Nebuchadrezzar's Great City

A cuneiform text has given archeologists a lot of information about the outline of the city, but it

*The Ishtar gate, built of glazed bricks, was taken from Babylon and is now in the Pergamon Museum in Berlin. The gate stood between the outer and inner walls of Babylon. The processional way ran through the gate to the sacred area of the city.*

*Nebuchadrezzar and his wife relax in the beautiful Hanging Gardens of Babylon. They are being fanned by servants and entertained by a court musician playing a harp. The king and queen wear embroidered garments decorated with sequins made of gold. They are enjoying drinks chilled with ice from the royal icehouse. An icehouse was found at the palace of Zimri-Lim at Mari dating from about 2000 BCE.*

was Nebuchadrezzar who rebuilt the city and turned it into a magnificent city. He rebuilt the temple of Marduk and the ziggurat. He also built the fabled Hanging Gardens of Babylon as a a gift for one of his wives, who had become very homesick for the mountains of her native Media. In order to protect the city of Babylon, Nebuchadrezzar built walls that encircled an area of more than 3 square miles (8 sq. km). He also took a major role in the Akitu festival that marked the Babylonian new year.

## NEO-BABYLONIAN KINGS

**The Chaldean Dynasty 625–562 BCE**

**625–605 BCE** Nabopolassar

**614 BCE** Destruction of Ashur

**612 BCE** Sack of Nineveh

**605–562 BCE** Nebuchadrezzar

**605 BCE** Defeat of Pharaoh Necho at Carchemish in Syria

**Kings of Judah, 640–587 BCE**

**640–609 BCE** Josiah

Josiah exploits Assyria's weakness to re-establish the Davidic kingdom, but he is killed in 609 BCE by Pharaoh Necho II at Meggido

**609–598 BCE** Jehoiakim

**598–597 BCE** Jehoiachin

**597 BCE** Jehoiachin deported to Babylon

**597–587 BCE** Zedekiah

**587 BCE** Siege of Jerusalem, destruction of the Temple, and deportation of citizens to Babylon

# Babylon

**At one time,** Babylon was the most magnificent city of the ancient world. Herodotus, the Greek historian, visited Babylon in

about 450 BCE and enthused about the city, saying, "Babylon surpasses in splendor any city of the known world."

Babylon was located in present-day Iraq, about 50 miles (80 km) south of Baghdad. It became important in the reign of Hammurabi (1792–1750 BCE). When Babylon refused to be taken over by the Assyrians, Sennacherib (705–681 BCE) destroyed the city. In the Neo-Babylonian era, Babylon became the capital of an empire. To reflect its position, both Nabopolassar and his son Nebuchadrezzar

(605–562 BCE) undertook huge building programs. When the Persians took control, Babylon continued to be an important city. The Persian ruler, Cyrus, arrived in Babylon in 539 BCE. The Persian kings made Babylon their winter capital. Alexander the Great (356–323 BCE) also came to Babylon without meeting any resistance. When his general Seleucus built a new capital further along the Tigris River, Babylon fell into permanent decline.

### "Gates of the Gods"

The name *Babylon* means "gate of the gods." The city, which was the shape of a rectangle, was defended by a double wall. There were eight gateways within the wall, each protected by its own god or goddess. The most spectacular of the gates was dedicated to Ishtar. It was decorated with brilliant blue tiles that had

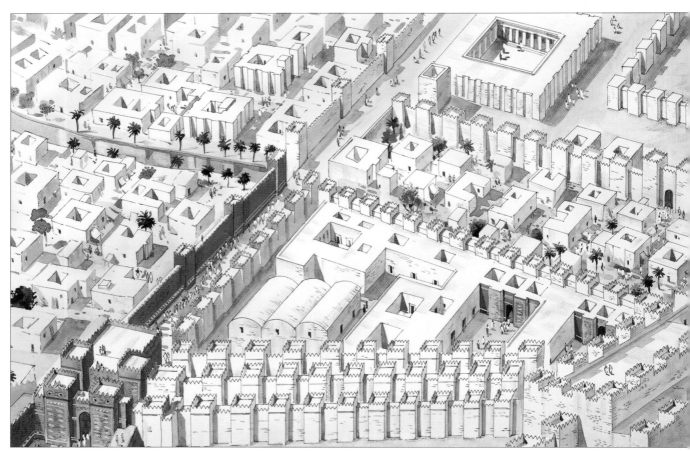

RIGHT: The Processional Way was decorated with some 120 lions—
symbols of Ishtar—depicted in glazed tiles. The Ishtar Gate also
pictured dragons and aurochs, a breed of cow that is now extinct.

pictures of bulls and dragons on them. The
processional way that ran through the gate led
to the great temple of Marduk and the ziggurat.

### The Hanging Gardens

Long considered as one of the seven wonders
of the ancient world, the Hanging Gardens of
Babylon were built by Nebuchadrezzar for his
wife Amityia. The sight of the gardens with
their beautiful plants must have been amazing
for travelers, who had traveled through desert
to reach the hot and dusty city. However, the
site of the famous gardens has never been
found. Nor has the Tower of Babel, which is
referred to in the Bible.

BELOW: Ancient Babylon covered an area of more than 2,150
acres (70 hectares)—larger than many modern towns. At the time
of Nebuchadrezzar, the Euphrates River flowed through the city,
dividing it into two sections, which were connected by a bridge. In
the older, eastern part (left) was the king's palace, near the Ishtar
gate (bottom left). From here, the processional way led toward
the great temple of Marduk and the ziggurat (top center). The
western part of Babylon (right) was probably a residential area.

# THE PERSIAN EMPIRE (560–521 BCE)

**Cyrus became king** of the Persians in 559 BCE. The Persians were then a relatively small group, but within a short period they conquered many of their neighbors. When Cyrus became king, the Median king Astyges was his overlord, while Croesus ruled Lydia and Nabonidus ruled Babylon. Cyrus conquered all three kings and founded the Persian Empire. The Persians would dominate West Asia for the next 200 years.

## The Conquests of Cyrus

Cyrus ruled between 559 and 530 BCE, during which time he became the most important ruler in the region. In 550 BCE, he turned against Astyges, the king of the Medes. The Medes had conquered the cities of Ashur, Kalhu, and Nineveh between 612 and 614 BCE, bringing an end to the Assyrian Empire. Cyrus marched to the Median capital of Hamadan, and took the wealth of the Medians and their vast empire that stretched from Turkey to Central Asia.

*This wall carving among the ruins of Persepolis show a lion attacking a horse. Above, a line of visiting ambassadors from subject territories climb a staircase with gifts to present to the Persian emperor.*

Next, Cyrus went after the Lydians. In 547 BCE, he led his armies to the western border of his empire. Croesus, the Lydian ruler, was known for his vast wealth. There was gold on Lydian land and the Lydians may have been the first people to use large numbers of gold coins. To prove their worth, these coins were stamped. Croesus controlled the Greek cities on the Aegean coast and when he heard of Cyrus' defeat of the Medes, he thought it was an opportunity to increase the Lydian Empire. Croesus traveled to seek advice from the oracle at Delphi, who prophesied a great empire would be destroyed. Croesus assumed it would be the Persian Empire—in fact, it was his own.

## Babylon: Jewel in Cyrus' Crown

When Nabonidus (555–539 BCE) came to the Babylonian throne, he was over 60 years old. He made his daughter the priestess of Sin at Ur and rebuilt the temple to Sin in Harran. It

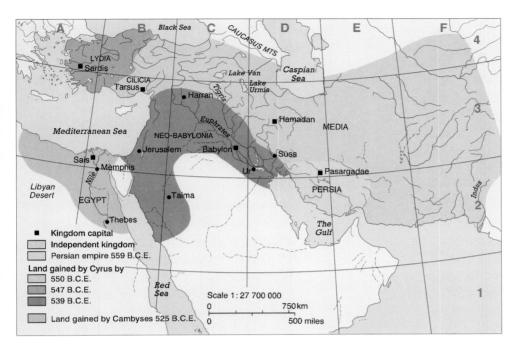

The growth of the Persian empire. Cyrus' vast lands stretched from the coast of the Mediterranean to the Indus valley. The Persians had been ruled by the Medes when Cyrus became king. Within a few years, he had conquered the territories of the Medes, which stretched to Central Asia in the east, the Babylonian lands in the south, and the Lydian kingdom, in modern Turkey, in the west. Cyrus' son Cambyses also controlled Egypt.

was not a good time for the Babylonians. Famine and plague ravaged the city. Then, for reasons we do not know, Nabonidus did not stay in Babylon but left for Taima, in northwest Arabia. His son, Belshazzar, ruled in his place, but since he was not officially the king, the city could not celebrate the Akitu, or New Year's festival, for 10 years.

The Babylonians did not like Nabonidus, because they felt he neglected the city's major deity, Marduk. In 539 BCE, the Akitu festival was once again celebrated, as described by both contemporary Greek historians and the Book of David in the Bible. This marked the end of the Babylonian dynasty. When Cyrus and his army arrived in Babylon in 539 BCE, they met no resistance. Cyrus instructed his men not to damage the city or its temples.

## Foundation of the Persian Empire

Cyrus called himself, "king of the world, great king ... king of Babylon, king of Sumer and Akkad." He was tolerant and allowed the Jews exiled in Babylon by Nebuchadrezzar to return home to Jerusalem and rebuild the Temple.

Cyrus used Lydian craftsmen to build his new capital at Pasargadae (now in modern Iran). They also built a massive tomb for him, where he was buried in 530 BCE, after being killed in battle in Central Asia.

Cambyses (529–522 BCE), the son of Cyrus, expanded the empire. Notably, he conquered Egypt in 525 B.E. Unlike his father, Cambyses had a reputation for being a tyrant. He lived in Egypt and behaved in many ways like a pharaoh. In 522 BCE, he left Egypt to return to Persia, but he died on the journey.

# DARIUS' EMPIRE (521–486 BCE)

**Darius became the** next ruler of the Persian Empire after Cambyses. Unlike Cambyses, Darius was a brilliant ruler. He expanded the Persian Empire all the way to Europe. However, he only came to the throne after a struggle.

## The Behistun Inscription

We know about the battle that Darius had to become king after Cambyses died in 522 BCE because of the famous inscription of Behistun. It was carved on a rock that overlooked the main caravan route from Babylon to Hamadan, in northern Iran. The inscription is carved in three languages—Old Persian, Babylonian, and Elamite. Archeologists have deciphered the inscription, which gives an account of the events surrounding the succession to the Persian throne.

According to Darius' account of events, a priest called Gaumata seized the throne, pretending to be Bardiya, the brother Cambyses murdered. Gaumata was accepted as king because nobody dared to challenge him until

Darius murdered him in 522 BCE. However, the truth is slightly different. In all probability, Darius most likely took the Persian throne by force from Bardiya. Although Darius did belong to the Achaemenid family, he was not the direct heir to the throne.

Following Cambyses' death, rebellions broke out in numerous places right across the Persian Empire. Within a year, Darius had established his rule over the kings of Persia, Elam, Media, Assyria, Egypt, Parthia, Margian, Sattagydia, and Scythia. Historians know about these victories from the relief that accompanies the Behistun inscription. The carving shows Darius under the winged standard of Ahura-Mazda, who was the main god of the Zoroastrian religion, receiving homage from the nine kings.

*Building materials for the palace at Susa. Darius made the city of Susa the capital of his huge empire. He imported materials from every corner of his territories to build his palace there. In 500 BCE, he built a canal from the Nile River to the Red Sea, making it much easier to bring goods by ship from Egypt. Darius was proud of the resources used and left inscriptions at Susa listing the people and the materials involved in building his palace.*

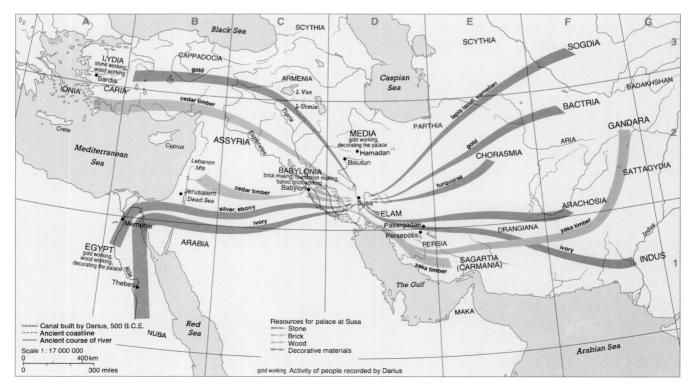

Darius believed that he had been chosen by the supreme god, Ahura-Mazda, to rule. He believed his kingship was a gift of the gods that he had to honor by helping his people. An inscription on his rock-cut tomb at Naqsh-i Rastam says that Darius was a friend to the good and an enemy to the evil. He protected the weak from the strong, and also the strong from the weak; he desired what was right; he was a good horseman, a good archer, and a good spearman.

## The Persian Empire Under Darius

Darius' empire stretched from Central Asia to Egypt. He divided his empire into 20 provinces, each with its own governor. Darius conquered the Indus region and in 513 BCE he fought against the Scythians in Thrace on the Black Sea. He went as far west as Europe, crossing the Danube River.

In 499 BCE, the Greeks, living in Cyprus and on the Aegean coast of Turkey, rebelled

*These glazed-brick archers from a wall of Darius' palace in Susa probably represent the king's Persian bodyguards (although their uniform may be those of Elamite soldiers). According to an inscription on the palace, the frieze was the work of craftsmen from Babylon, where brick reliefs were used extensively.*

against the Persians. The rebellion lasted six years. Darius was able to regain control of Cyprus with the help of the Phoenician navy, but he found that the Greek cities on the Turkish coast were harder to control. In 494 BCE, the Persian naval fleet of 600 ships proved to be too strong for the smaller Greek navy in a sea battle off the island of Lade, near Miletus. Darius then tried to take mainland Greece, but the Greek army defeated the Persian army at Marathon in 490 BCE.

When Darius died in 486 BCE, his son, Xerxes, inherited a well-organized empire. It had a taxation system, as well as efficient communications that kept the furthest reaches of the empire in touch with the capital by using horseback messengers to rely messages.

# Susa

**Susa is located**

on the plains of Khuzestan in southwest Iran. It was founded in about 4000 BCE as a religious center.
In about 2500 BCE, the city was the capital of Elam, the territory of which sometimes stretched into the Fars region and to Anshan in the southeast. With the rise of the dynasty of Agade in 2300 BCE, Susa came under Mesopotamian control. In 2004 BCE, it was reunited with Anshan, beginning the Elamite era. Almost 800 years later, in one of the most brilliant periods of their history, the Elamites overran Mesopotamia. They destroyed the cities of Babylonia and Assyria, and brought their finest art treasures as war booty to Susa.

## Ashurbanipal's Anger

Elamite interference in Babylonia angered the Assyrian rulers. In about 647 BCE, after numerous failed attempts, Ashurbanipal (668–627 BCE) captured Susa. He burned the city and destroyed its temples and sacred grovies. He they plowed salt into the fields so that no crops could grow—an ancient method of chemical warfare.

## City of Darius

The time of the Persian empire was a golden period for Susa. The city blossomed under Darius the Great (522–486 BCE), who made it his administrative capital. On the Apadana mound of the city he built a large palace, combining Babylonian and Median architecture. Workers and luxury materials were brought from all parts of the Persian empire, including cedar wood

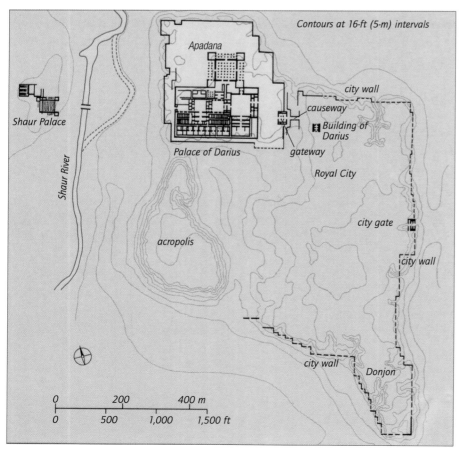

*The site of Susa, which was identified in 1851 CE, has four mounds. Three of them—the palace, the acropolis or "high place," which was the main religious center, and the royal city—belong to the period of the Persian empire.*

*This brick relief of a lion decorated the walls of Darius' palace at Susa.*

from the Lebanon Mountains. Darius employed renowned craftsmen to decorate the palace. A statue of the king found in the palace gatehouse, for example, was carved in Egypt and brought to Susa, probably by boat. Darius' palace is mentioned in the biblical books of Esther and Nehemiah, where the city is called Shushan.

## Alexander the Great

Alexander the Great captured Susa in 331 BCE. To cement his empire together, he arranged the mass marriage of Greek soldiers and Persian women there. Even after the fall of the Persian empire, Susa remained an important city. Marked by an unusual white stone cone, the tomb of the biblical prophet Daniel is through to be near the acropolis area (now the village of Shush) and is still visited by Muslim pilgrims, for whom Daniel is also an important prophet.

*This Islamic vase, from the eighth or ninth centuries CE, was found at Susa, where it was probably left by a visiting Muslim pilgrim to the tomb of Daniel.*

**The last years** of the Persian empire were a time of increasing struggle with the Greeks, who were becoming a growing power in the eastern Mediterranean. The Persians gained some early victories, but they were followed by defeats.

## Xerxes against the Greeks

Darius' son Xerxes (486–465 BCE) was his chosen successor. According to Herodotus, the ancient Greek historian, Xerxes spent years preparing for war against the Greeks. Then, in 480 BCE, he led two million men in an invasion of Greece. They crossed the narrow strait at the Dardanelles on bridges made from boats. The Persians marched south, easily defeating brave but ineffectual Spartan resistance at the battle of Thermopylae. Xerxes' soldiers captured Athens while, according to Herodotus, the king "looked on from under a golden canopy." However, the Greek navy defeated the Persian fleet at the battle of Salamis. Xerxes returned to Persia, leaving his army in winter quarters in northern Greece and one of his generals, Mardonius, in command. The following year, Mardonius again captured Athens briefly, but he was killed in a heavy Persian defeat in a land battle at Plataia in 479 BCE. The Persian armies left Greece, but

they were again heavily defeated, this time at Mycale in Ionia.

## Murder in the Persian Court

The defeats in Greece marked a turning point. It was clear that the Persian army was no longer invincible and that the Persian navy no longer ruled the seas. However, Greece was only peripheral to the main part of the Persian empire. It remained intact and at peace until Xerxes died in 465 BCE. Some 60 years later, a Greek physician working at the Persian court, recorded that Xerxes had been assassinated by three of his courtiers, including the Grand Vizier.

The Persian court ow entered a period of plots and multiple murders, often by poisoning. One of Xerxes' three sons, Artaxerxes I, killed his oldest brother Darius and seized the throne. Then, in 425 BCE, three of Xerxes' grandsons ruled in quick succession, the first two being murdered after only a few months on the

*The empire of Alexander the Great. When Alexander defeated Darius III at Gaugamela in 331 BCE, he became lord of all the Persian territories, which extended to Central Asia and India. When he died at the age of 33, his generals divided up the vast kingdom between them. West Asia went to Seleucus, while Egypt was governed by Ptolemy.*

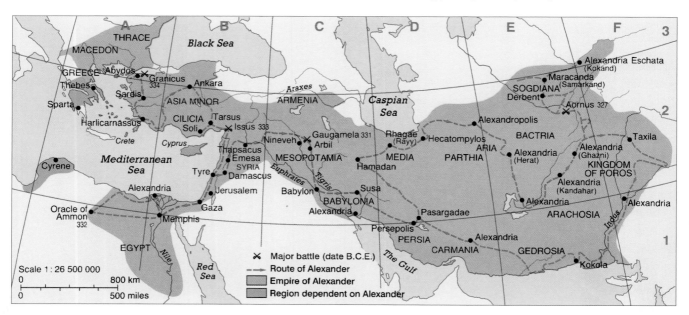

throne. More royal conspiracies, murders, and civil wars followed for a period of almost 100 years, as rival successors tried to establish a firm grip on the throne by eliminating any source of potential opposition.

## Darius III and Alexander

Darius III (335–330 BCE) survived all the palace plots to take the throne, but in 334 BCE he found himself facing a far greater problem. King Alexander had been on the throne of Macedon, in northern Greece, for two years. Now Alexander, better known today as Alexander the Great, led his army against the Persian empire. Alexander's troops defeated those of Darius at Granicus in 334 BCE and then at Issus in 335 BCE. Alexander, who meanwhile had also invaded Egypt, had not set out to conquer the whole of the Persian empire, but with each victory his troops advanced into Persian territory and his ambitions grew. In 331 BCE, after another defeat at the battle of Gaugamela near the ancient city of Nineveh, Darius fled from the battlefield, only to be killed by his own courtiers.

*A relief of a Persian soldier from Persepolis. The Persian defeats in Greece in the late fifth century BCE were the first sign that the once invincible empire was growing weaker. It remained intact, however, until Alexander the Great invaded about 150 years later.*

Alexander took command of the entire Persian empire. He now ruled the great cities of Babylon, Susa, Persepolis, and Hamadan. Persepolis was destroyed by fire, either by accident or as a deliberate policy by Alexander. The fire was highly symbolic. The empire of Cyrus and Darius, which had survived for 150 years was at an end, and so was the great civilization of ancient West Asia.

*Alexander the Great (356–323 BCE) leads his armies on a campaign. His conquests stretched from Macedonia and Greece to the Indus River in Asia. In battle against the Indian king Porhates, Alexander crossed the Indus. His army defeated the Indians, whose elephants panicked in battle. But Alexander's Greek troops were homesick and refused to advance further, so he began the long march back to Greece. Reaching Babylon in 323 BCE, Alexander, the invincible warrior, caught a fever and soon died.*

# GLOSSARY

## A

**Aceramic** A term given to the Neolithic period (c.8500–7000 BCE) before pottery was invented.

**Akkad** The northern part of Mesopotamia. The southern area was called Sumer. Akkad was named after the city Agade, but by about 1800 BCE the region was called Babylonia.

**Akkadian** The dynasty founded by Sargon (c.2300 BCE). Also the name of a Semitic language that was spoken in Mesopotamia as early as 3000 BCE.

**Anatolia** The highland plains of present-day central Turkey.

**Assyria** The northern part of modern Iraq, near the border with Turkey.

**Assyrian** A dialect of Akkadian spoken by the Assyrians. Also the name of a dynasty that has three main periods (c.2000–612 BCE).

## B

**Babylonia** The region of southern Mesopotamia that was called Akkad before about 1800 BCE.

**Babylonian** A dialect of Akkadian spoken by Babylonians. Also the name of the dynasty that ruled from about 2000 BCE to 750 BCE.

## C

**cuneiform** The wedge-shaped script of Akkadian that was written on clay tablets and was used throughout Mesopotamia and the Near East.

## D

**diorite** A very hard black stone that was used to make statues.

**dynasty** A line of rulers usually from a single family or related through marriage.

## E

**Epi-Paleolithic** The continuation of the Paleolithic or Old Stone Age culture after the last Ice Age. This period, which is sometimes called the Mesolithic, was followed by the Neolithic period.

## F

**Fertile Crescent** The lands between the highland zones of Turkey and Iran and the deserts of Arabia, having 8 inches (20 cm) of rainfall each year.

**figurine** A small statue made from wood, ivory, clay, or metal.

**flint** A hard stone used to make tools in the Paleolithic, Epi-Paleolithic, and Neolithic periods.

## K

**king list** A list of the names of kings and the lengths of their reigns. The best known is the Sumerian King List, which records the dynasties ruling the cities of Sumer until 2000 BCE.

## L

**lapis lazuli** A semiprecious blue stone that is found only in the mountains of Afghanistan.

**law code** A collection of laws recording the penalties for different crimes. The best-known law code is that of Hammurabi (c.1800 BCE).

**Levant** The lands bordering the eastern Mediterranean, now modern Lebanon, Israel, and coastal Syria.

## M

**Mesolithic** The Middle Stone Age period between the Paleolithic, or Old Stone Age and the Neolithic, or New Stone Age. Also known as the Epi-Paleolithic.

**Mesopotamia** A Greek word meaning "between the rivers" and describing the lands in present-day Iraq, from south of modern Baghdad to the Persian Gulf. The northern part of Mesopotamia was called Akkad, the southern lands Sumer.

**microliths** Very small chipped stone tools that first appear in the Mesolithic period.

## N

**Natufian** A culture of the Epi-Paleolithic period in the Levant (c.11,000–9300 BCE) when people began to grow grain.

**Neolithic** The New Stone Age (c.9300–4000 BCE), which was divided into the Proto-Neolithic and Aceramic periods.

## O

**obsidian** A natural volcanic glass from Anatolia that is much sharper than flint and was used to make tools.

## P

**Paleolithic** The Old Stone Age, which ended with the last Ice Age in about 12,000 BCE People obtained their food by hunting and gathering during this period.

**pharaoh** The title of the king of ancient Egypt.

**Proto-Neolithic** The period during the New Stone Age when grain was first grown (c.9000–8500 BCE).

## S

**Semitic** The language family that was widely spoken in Mesopotamia and the Near East and includes Akkadian and its dialects, Assyrian and Babylonian.

**stele** An upright stone or wooden slab, often decorated with carvings or bearing inscriptions.

**Sumer** The southern lands of Mesopotamia, reaching the Persian Gulf, that were occupied by the Sumerians. The plain north of modern Baghdad was called Akkad.

**Sumerian** The language that was spoken in Sumer by the Sumerians in about 4000 BCE Sumerian does not belong to the Semitic language family.

## T

**tablet** A small flat slab, usually made of clay, on which an inscription in cuneiform would be written.

**tell** An Arabic word for a mound made by the remains of ancient settlements. Often part of a place name, as in Tell Madhhur.

## Z

**ziggurat** A high tower built in stepped stages with a temple at the top.

# FURTHER RESOURCES

## PUBLICATIONS

Bahrani, Z. *Women of Babylon: Gender and Representation in Mesopotamia* (Routledge, 2001).

Charvet, P. *Mesopotamia Before History* (Routledge, 2002).

Collon, D. *Ancient Near Eastern Art* (British Museum Press, 1995).

Crawford, H. *Sumer and the Sumerians* (Cambridge University Press, 2004).

Curtis, J. *Ancient Persia* (British Museum Press, 2000).

Gruber, Beth. *Ancient Iraq: National Geographic Investigates* (National Geographic Society, 2007).

Gurney, O. R. *The Hittites* (Viking Penguin, 1991).

Leick, G. *Mesopotamia: The Invention of the City* (Penguin, 2000).

Matthews, R. *The Archaeology of Mesopotamia: Theories and Approaches* (Routledge, 2003).

McIntosh, J. *Ancient Mesopotamia: New Perspectives* (ABC–CLIO, 2005).

Nicolle, D. *History of Medieval Life* (Chancellor Press, 1997).

Oakes, L., and P. Steele. *Everyday Life in Ancient Egypt and Mesopotamia* (Southwater, 2006).

Oates, J. C. *Babylon* (Thames & Hudson, 1986).

Perce, A. *Art of the Ancient Near East* (Harry N. Abrams, 1980).

Pollock, S. *Ancient Mesopotamia* (Cambridge University Press, 1999).

Roaf, M. *Cultural Atlas of Mesopotamia and the Ancient Near East* (Facts On File, 1990).

Roux, G. *Ancient Iraq* (Viking Penguin, 1993).

Schomp, V. *Ancient Mesopotamia: The Sumerians, Babylonians, and Assyrians* (Franklin Watts, 2005).

Schuster, A. M. M., and M. Polk (eds.). *The Looting of the Iraq Museum: The Lost Legacy of Mesopotamia* (Harry N. Abrams, 2005).

Tubb, J. *Bible Lands* (Dorling Kindersley, 1991).

## WEBSITES

http://www.baghdadmuseum.org/home.php
The Iraq National Museum in Baghdad.

http://www.crystalinks.com/mesopotamia.html
Sections on climate, government, history, language, art, and religion.

http://www.mesopotamia.co.uk
British Museum Website coverage of the history and culture of ancient Mesopotamia.

http://oi.uchicago.edu/OI/UR/Ur_home.html
Site about the excavation of the Royal Tombs of Ur, hosted by the Oriental Institute at the University of Chicago.

http://www.wsu.edu/~dee/MESO/MESO.htm
Washington State University's Mesopotamia Website.

# INDEX